TEACHII
TO THINK

*My Year of Dog Agility Training
with My Collie, Willow*

———

KIMBERLY DAVIS

Climbing Ivy Press
Hingham, MA USA

CLIMBING IVY PRESS
Hingham, MA USA

ISBN-10: 0983449201
ISBN-13: 9780983449201
Library of Congress Control Number: 2011925010
Climbing Ivy Press, Hingham, MA

Front cover photograph used by permission of Jonathan Simmons.
Copyright © 2000 Jonathan Simmons.

Author photograph used by permission of Trudy Tucker.
Copyright © 2004 Trudy Tucker.

For permissions and reprints, please contact:
Climbing Ivy Press, P.O. Box 199, Hingham, MA 02043.

For Steve and Daniel

Preface and Acknowledgment

Eight years ago, when I began taking dog agility classes with my collie Willow, I had no idea that for a time agility training would come to take over my life. As far as I was concerned, I was just signing up for more obedience classes with the unruly family dog. During that period, I was on an extended hiatus from practicing law, a career I had left a few years earlier to care for my dying mother and my young son. My mother had recently passed on, though, and my son had reached an age where he was in school part of the day, leaving me suddenly—and for the first time in my adult life—with free time on my hands, time that I used to pursue my MFA in creative writing and to take up dog agility. Little did I know that agility training would turn out to have a profound effect upon me. I am still working out in my own mind all that I took from the training. Certainly agility has dramatically changed the way I look at animals. When I started, I think that I viewed the family pets mainly as infantile creatures—as wayward simpletons I needed to boss and control in order to make them more docile, tractable, and pleasant to be around. No real interchange with them was required or even especially desirable. I now see the family pets—and particularly my dogs—very differently. I understand them as fully matured and fledged individual personalities with their own needs and desires—desires that we humans can harness to get more out of them than would ever be possible through the old "forced" training methods I used to use. But that is not the only thing that I took from agility. In addition to revealing things about the animals in my care, the training also showed me a great deal about myself, especially about my interpersonal relationships and how I conducted myself in the world—and particularly the shortcomings in the way I was parenting my son, Daniel. Through the training I gained valuable lessons about how to get others to do what you want, about teaching and learning and building skills, and about fostering creativity. I have, for the most part, disguised the identities of the agility trainers with whom Willow and I worked to protect their privacy, but they know who they are. To these talented teachers, I am deeply indebted. They have enriched my life and deepened my understanding of dogs and of humans in more ways than I can count. My hope is that this little book will serve as something of a valentine to these calm, sane, and remarkable people from whom I have learned so much.

Kimberly Davis
October 2008

Motivation is the art of getting people to do what you want them to do because they want to do it.

—Dwight D. Eisenhower

I. Relinquishing Force

One

This story has its beginning on an evening in mid-September, 2000. I had arrived with my dog just before dark at the equestrian arena in Plymouth, Massachusetts, where our first agility class would be held. Not yet aware that there was parking behind the arena, I had left our car up by the road, and we now made our way on foot down the long sloping gravel drive toward the big blue dome-shaped building. At the time, I had very little information about agility. I knew only that it was the newest rage in dog sports in the United States, and that it involved a course of varying obstacles through which the dogs raced, performing jumps, tunnels, seesaws, and balance beams. Years later, as I write this, you can catch at least a glimpse of agility nearly any night on Animal Planet, but at the time we began our training I had only read about this burgeoning sport of dog antics in magazines, and seen a demonstration or two at dog shows. It looked like fun to me, and having already done a little obedience training, I had decided to give it a try with my yearling collie, Willow.

And so we crunched down the long gravel driveway, my dog and me, through the gathering dusk to the arena. It was, as I recall, still summer warm that evening, tiny insects raining upon my bare arms, and the fading light growing misty over scrubby pines. We were not far from the ocean, and the air smelled strongly of salt. As we walked, Willow strained at the end of his taut webbed leash, his neck clicking the links of his choke collar and his nose twitching with the musky, exciting scent of hot horse on the hoof. I had gotten this dog as a puppy from a highly recommended breeder in Danbury, Connecticut, and dancing this way at the end of his lead he looked—at the time—every bit the specimen of a lovely purebred collie.

Now when I say that Willow was (and is) a purebred collie, I don't mean the picture that—after some recent children's movies—vaults to a lot of people's minds: of a small nervous piebald dog crouched before a bunch of sheep, riveting them with his gaze. That would be the border collie. That is not Willow. Willow is what people used to think of as a collie back in the glory days of Hollywood when the word meant Lassie and Lad and other such leggy, blond canines. Willow is what these days is called a "rough collie," and he is firmly in that *Lassie Come Home* line. He was then—and though older, remains today— a tall, elegant, golden dog with a deep white chest and tiny almond-shaped eyes set into a long flat head. *With slightly crossed eyes*, you might think, were you to look at him straight on, for he has that highly bred cast of British royalty. But he was, and is, handsome anyway—and back then he was extremely pleasing to look at, especially in motion—with his high-stepping show-ring gait. He was that night, in short, a gorgeous exemplar of his kind. He was everything that the American Kennel Club might have dreamed up for a young purebred collie. But at a year old, he was also a boisterous youngster, and deeply unruly despite months of "Puppy Kindergarten" classes. And he had always wanted to chase and bring down a full-sized horse.

He just never knew it until that moment when he actually saw one for the first time.

A big caramel-colored thoroughbred had come sidestepping out of the mouth of the arena and directly across the gravel path in front of us. Willow's reaction was immediate and enthusiastic. He reared back on his hind legs and lunged forward at the skittish equine, exerting maximum pressure on his choke collar and leash, and nearly yanking me off my feet. I am a small, book-oriented woman, and even with the choke collar he and I were nearly an even match. In the same moment as he jerked forward, Willow also gathered into that deep white chest of his a great gasp of air that was released as shrill, rapid-fire barking ending in something resembling a howl as the choke collar throttled his windpipe with a zipping noise. Struggling to reassert my authority over my hysterical charge, while not actually strangling him, I grasped my hand through the flat, webbed collar he also wore, and snapped the leash onto this kinder restraint from which his dog tags swung like a necklace. Willow bounced on his forepaws, still barking shrilly at the horse, but I had him now, and I led him firmly by the collar around the corner of the building and into the corrugated-aluminum arena.

The thing that initially struck me upon entering an equestrian arena for the first time was the sheer sense of space. It seemed a huge area to be housed indoors, almost as large as an indoor football field, a truly enormous expanse to be cordoned off from the outside, especially—I thought—out here in the middle of nowhere—in the dark pine forests of Boston's South Shore halfway to Cape Cod. The floor of the great barn was entirely covered with a fine brown sawdust that looked as if it might have fallen as dandruff from that tall thoroughbred outside. The sawdust was that same rich brown horse color, rolling out in front of my feet like a deep-pile carpet. My second impression, once my eyes had adjusted to the great space, was that of a very odd yard sale going on inside the arena, for strange brightly painted furniture was scattered about the floor in clusters. After a moment, and with closer scrutiny, the odd furniture resolved itself into equally strange playground equipment. There were jumps and balance beams and tunnels. Spare tires and seesaws and ladders laid on the ground. And straight lines of upright poles, the kind you might see marking holes at a golf course, but seven or eight of them lined up in a row. These and other such apparatus littered the floor of the huge barn, suggesting—what?—a dog party out of Dr. Seuss? Dogs swinging on swings, dogs riding on seesaws, dogs sailing through the air or climbing in trees? Actually, I recall at the time there was a black and white springer spaniel weaving its taut body through a set of poles with alarming speed. This would turn out to be our instructor's beautifully trained agility dog, who would retire to a crate once class started.

Several other dog training students—human and canine— arrived more or less at the same time as Willow and me, and once we were all inside the arena, we were greeted by a tall trim woman with dark bobbed hair, maybe in her late forties, who introduced herself as Sue Reed, our instructor for this fall agility class. Sue was the reason that Willow and I had driven the twenty minutes down Route 3 from our home in Marshfield, Massachusetts, having found her name recommended on an agility website. She's upper crusty, this one, I remember thinking as she greeted us, giving equal attention to the dogs and the humans. She spoke pleasantly to us between clenched teeth under heavy cheekbones—like William F. Buckley, I thought. Straight legged, athletic, and lithe, there was an easy grace to her movements. She had the manner of one who has never known cares or had to raise her voice. This, I would quickly come to understand, was something of a false first impression. Sue would prove neither especially rich nor high-toned. She spoke with a thicker Boston accent than I first appreciated, and after class would load her tuxedo-coated springers into a dinged-up subcompact. I think what impressed me upon meeting her was her air of calm, imperturbable authority, something one ordinarily associates with the well to do. It is something that I have since noticed successful animal trainers often seem to have, and something I myself sorely lack. Another trainer Willow and I later worked with would regularly say to me, "Look, you must learn to calm down. Don't get so excited." Sue would soon be calling out to us to "stand up straight, take your hands out of your pockets, arms relaxed at your sides." Despite these well-intended words, I doubt now that a relaxed posture is something that can be counseled. The calm, natural authority of the true animal trainer is, I now suspect, something inborn. I would spend my months of agility training mainly in a bent kneed crouch, as if ready to flee at any moment, my body wracked by nervous twitches and fast uncertain gestures as we labored to master our complex maneuvers.

After introducing herself, Sue glanced about with a sort of mild disapproval at her new dog agility pupils. There were by now six or seven handlers gathered in front of her with our dogs of varying breeds. Sue began by stating her training principles in a clear, ringing tone, as if to the recalcitrant or merely ignorant. "We will have no negative training," she said. "Agility is not obedience training. It is fun and games for the dogs. Fun and games. We will not be using choke collars." (At this point, Sue was walking up and down in front of her row of agility students rather like a drill sergeant.) "There will be no jerking of the dogs' necks," she continued. "No pushing the dogs around. We will not reprimand the dogs with 'no.' No saying 'oops' or 'uh-oh' if your dog makes a mistake."

As she said these last few things, Sue was gazing at me, it seemed, and wearing a bland, slightly mystified expression. I was conscious, suddenly, of what I was doing with my own dog. Willow had started barking again with the excitement of all the other arriving dogs and handlers, and I had clicked his leash back on his choke collar and had been snapping his neck with this chain link noose to quiet him the whole time Sue had been speaking. "No," I had told him several times, in a loud stage whisper. Sue had now paused in her introductory remarks and was cocking an eyebrow at me. She said, in a voice laced with irony, "Do you have a flat buckle collar?" (She could see that I did.) *Then why don't you use it,* was what she didn't add. *And didn't I just say to quit jerking his neck?*

"I only put the choke collar on because of the horses and the other dogs," I explained to her weakly, at the same time clicking Willow's leash back on his flat webbed collar. "He gets so excited." But I did not remove the steel choke from around his neck.

Sue eyed me coldly with her icy blue eyes, and then moved on to another handler whose border collie was wearing a harness. When she was done checking our collars, she stepped back and said, in that same ringing instructor's voice, "In here, we reward the good behavior and ignore the bad. We are teaching the dogs to think. Teaching the dogs to think." She repeated this phrase as if it was a mystery we were to ponder.

Teaching the dogs to think, huh?

This idea was new to me. That dogs might be able to think. That they might be capable of rational thought. I had never especially thought of dogs as thinking. At the time, I couldn't imagine what Sue was talking about. I gazed down skeptically at Willow.

Under Sue's scrutiny, my young collie had quieted for a few moments, but he was now back to barking again, bounding on his front paws, still excited by all the new smells. He had also seen, and—from our previous "Puppy Kindergarten" classes—apparently recognized, some of the agility equipment. We had practiced tunnels and jumps in our earlier training classes, and Willow knew that once he had whooshed through the long curving red tunnel or hopped over a low bar jump, he would get a tasty treat. He could also smell the commercially manufactured dog treats in the foil wrapper inside my jeans pocket. Seeing me looking down at him, he prodded the denim fabric covering the treats at my hip with his long velvet nose, and kept up his shrill racket.

"Can't you shut him up?" the woman next to me said, shooting me a dirty look. She was holding the leash of a sweet-faced sheltie with a ragged coat who was sitting attentively at her heel in a neat sit, absolutely silent.

"Sorry," I said, and resisted the urge to jerk Willow by the neck again.

What I normally would have done—which is to say what I had always been taught to do and therefore always had done, since I trained my first border collie at age nine—was to give my dog's neck hard and painful jerks with his choke collar and tell him several loud and firm *no*'s. If this didn't work, the next step would be a "stare down," which would involve taking him by the scruff of his neck, making him face me as I leaned into his eyes, and threatening him with certain death and dismemberment at the hands of me, his alpha bitch, if he didn't shut up and do as I say. This was how I had always trained my series of dogs, mostly collies. This was how most people always trained their dogs, until fairly recently, when more humane, behaviorally based training methods that go under the names "positive reinforcement" and "operant conditioning" came onto the dog training scene. Originally developed by dolphin trainers, who naturally couldn't use choke collar and leash, these new training methods had been widely transferred to the higher levels of dog training since approximately the early 1990s. It was a trend of which I had been blissfully ignorant until that moment. Old habits die hard, and I had been training with the harsh, punitive tactics for many years. Since I was nine years old, as I have said. Still, my old training methods were plainly verboten in this dog agility class, under Sue Reed's vigilant eye.

With a sigh of resignation, I reached into my pocket, doing the only other thing that I could think of doing at the moment to make my dog stop barking. It was something I had been taught to do in our previous obedience class where Willow also did a fair amount of barking and lunging. I decided to distract or "redirect him," as they say in dog training parlance, with a game of *earn the cookie*. It was a game that had always worked well with Willow. He has always been happy, more than happy actually, to work for dog treats. I pulled a tasty treat from the foil packet at my hip and held it out in front of his nose. Instantly he stopped lunging and yapping, and his long snout swiveled toward me, his brown eyes bright with interest, his ears pricked. I brought the dog treat to my chin and said, "Watch me." Willow's gaze found mine, his expression full of adoration (not for me perhaps, but for the treat). "Good watch me," I praised, and handed him the treat, and then pulled another from my pocket. "Now sit," I told him, and held the second treat out over his head. He looked at me, as he finished chewing the first treat, and then cast his gaze around at the other dogs, whose presence he had not forgotten. "Sit," I repeated and fingered the second treat. He looked back at me, deciding whether or not he would cooperate, and then sat. From his sitting position, he nuzzled my hand and then looked back at my face. "Down," I said and held the second treat low. He went down on his belly, and I handed the treat to him. Lying there, chewing quietly on his dog treat, Willow looked truly relaxed and calm for the first time that evening. It will probably not be lost on the reader that this reward/distraction method had worked far better for me than all of the shouting "no" and jerking on his collar that I previously did. What I need to add here, though, what I have left out of this picture, is the frustration I felt at that moment.

The fact is, *I didn't want* to reward Willow for *not barking*. What I wanted to do was to choke him into submission. The awful truth (and a truth I can admit to only in hindsight) is that there is a grim satisfaction in disciplining an animal or a small child and bending him to your will. It is a rather ugly satisfaction, and one that few people will acknowledge—though most have probably felt it at some time or another. The truth is, at that moment, what I really wanted to do was to jerk Willow's collar really hard, shout at him, grab him by his scruff, and stare or strangle him into obedience. I wanted to control him. I wanted to dominate him. I wanted him to behave *because I said so*. I would have liked him to be terrified of me, not all the time, but when *he knew he was thwarting my will,* or so I thought of it then. I probably rationalized that I was shaping his character or teaching him "good habits," but the truth is I wanted to see him crouched beside me in training, ears down at my heel, utterly obedient. This is how most people have always treated their work animals, and often their children as well for that matter. Discipline is part of our Christian worldview. And our domination of the animals has its biblical basis, does it not? In Genesis. For we humans are to have dominion over all the beasts of the earth. But, no, to say this is to excuse the unsavory emotions that accompanied this sentiment. I wanted to dominate Willow not for some vague, abstract reason, but because it would *feel good to me*. Not just good, satisfying. Vindicating. I didn't want him to work for treats. *I wanted him to mind.*

Since Willow was now relaxing and couldn't bark with his mouth full, I had a moment to look around me at the other dogs in the agility class and their owners for the first time that night. This was an interesting group, I remember thinking, the horsey-doggie set, not the family pets that we had seen at our town's obedience classes. These dogs were, for the most part, obviously gorgeous purebreds, and I would soon learn that several of the human students were dog breeders who were doing this as a way to add to their dogs' show titles and prestige. Many of the dogs were non-neutered or "intact," which may have accounted for some of Willow's excitement at their smell. The woman beside me with the sweet-faced sheltie boasted of the show titles her "bitch" had won, and then shook her head in despair. "She's a wreck," she said. "She blew her coat after she had her litter this summer. Now look at her." The woman's disapproval of her little sheltie's ragged coat only thinly disguised her evident pride. Her pretty-faced charge probably was indeed a successful show dog, I knew, since "expression" is one of the most sought-after attributes in shelties and collies, and this little dog's face was adorably symmetrical and puppyish.

In the class, there was also a stylish pair of women in their early thirties with a brace of snappy-looking black and white border collies. One of the border collies—a female—held her head low and gave us a hard, dangerous stare as we passed her on our way to the first piece of equipment we would try, the accordion-like tunnel. We'll keep away from that one, I thought, though Sue assured us that all of the dogs in the class had been "vetted for stability." Still, she admitted, some of them had "face issues," and she advised us to keep our own dogs' noses away from the other dogs. "Face issues" would quickly prove something of an understatement, since the border collie bitch would try to take a chunk out of any dog that came near her. I would soon learn that many of these agility dogs were selected for their high drive and compulsiveness, and that such traits often came with a certain level of nastiness, if not outright viciousness. As a result, you didn't see the kind of socializing in agility class that you often saw at obedience or Puppy-K classes. On our way to the tunnel, we met a young girl of no more than fifteen or sixteen with another sheltie, this one a bit fat and not nearly as pretty as the first. The girl told me that she was in the handling and show-judging program run by the Plymouth County 4-H. She looked curiously at Willow's head and remarked, "Collies have no stop," whatever that meant— some comment on the conformation of my dog's head, I supposed. There was also a gleaming black and white basset hound with a bass howl handled by a taciturn man who would turn out to be the president of the South Shore Dog Training Club. And there was a huge intact male Rottweiler manhandled by a muscular blond woman in a tight sparkly pink T-shirt. Now and then a low thunderous rumble issued from the Rottweiler's direction. I guessed that he had "face issues," too.

There was only one mutt in this crowd of fancy purebreds, a sort of enormous shaggy terrier-type with a baleful look, whose owner told me he was a cross of Irish wolfhound and pit bull. This sounded to me like a "what do you get when you cross a" joke, and I laughed out loud as the owner told me this and then apologized when his face took on a pained expression. He already knew his dog was funny looking and didn't need to be reminded. I remember gazing down at Willow and feeling glad that he was a pretty purebred. He truly was a stunning dog to look at, as several of the other handlers had already told me, to my great and overweening pleasure. He was from a long and distinguished line of champion collies, and no one in the class needed to know that he was banned from the show ring by the unfortunate occurrence of an undescended testicle, making him ineligible as breeding stock. Willow saw me looking at him, wagged his tail, and started barking again, and then we were back to the game of *watch the cookie*.

Willow remained excited and itching to go, even as I distracted him with treats. He kept lunging forward, wanting to dash through the tunnel and then move on to the jumps that we could see standing nearby. But the progress of the first night's class was achingly slow. The dogs stood in line, some patiently, some not, waiting to be introduced by Sue and their handlers to the apparatus. After the dogs were acquainted with the tunnel, one of the easiest pieces of equipment they would meet, and had whooshed through it a few times, they were shown to a ladder laid on the ground that they were asked to step through. The ladder would not be part of an eventual agility course, but was only to "show the dogs where their back legs were" before we went on to the next and more difficult piece of equipment, the long low balance beam, which later would turn into the high-soaring "dogwalk" several feet off the ground.

At last we reached the long plank, which at this point stood about knee high. The dogs were supposed to mount it at one end and then walk the full length without jumping off. The plank was about twelve feet long and ten inches wide. Ten inches sounds like a lot, but the plank was stationed nearly a foot above the earth, and while many of the dogs were happy to place their front feet on it, they balked at stepping up with their hind legs. Some of them jumped over the board; some put up their front paws and walked along it with their back feet still walking on *terra firma*. Sue explained that their reluctance was due to the fact that most dogs, especially the larger, longer-bodied ones, had no idea where their back legs were. That was the point of having them walk through the ladder first. To show them what was back there, at their rear ends. Only the two little shelties walked the plank happily and without a struggle. "The plank looks wider to the smaller dogs," Sue explained. And, of course, shelties were naturally agile. Sue wouldn't push or pull the reluctant dogs onto the plank, instead tempting them up slowly with treats. First one paw up and then another. Each bit of progress was lavishly rewarded. "It has to be their idea," she said. "They have to *decide* to do it." It was enough the first night for a dog to put up his front paws, if that's all he could manage.

It was more than not pushing and pulling the dogs, I thought, as I watched the painstaking progress of those ahead of us in line. Sue wouldn't allow the dogs to be lifted up and positioned on the plank, not even just to show them what to do. Not even for the smaller dogs. No dog's foot was to be placed up on the plank by a human. The dog had to come up with the idea for himself. What's the big deal with showing them what to do, I wondered, not getting it. How are they supposed to figure it out? That's what I thought at first. Then, as time went by, I thought, oh, good grief, this class is too big for this approach.

The class was supposed to be limited to six or seven dogs, but it now seemed to me that there must be at least nine or ten. (There were, due to some late arrivals. I counted.) And most of them were ahead of Willow in line, since I had hung back as a result of our little barking problem. Sue's method seemed to take forever. It was a matter, apparently, of waiting the dogs out. Waiting while each dog decided to try something different in order to get at the treats in the human hands. Some of the dogs were quicker to try things than the others. Some were dead slow. In each case, there were rewards for even incremental progress. Sue counseled patience. One paw up on the board, and then two. She did have some limited success—I had grudgingly to admit—but, really, it took forever and hardly seemed worth it. Wasn't there a faster way? Willow kept on barking, not understanding the delay. I kept redirecting him. Sit. Paw. Other paw. Down. Sit. Down. Sit. Down. Sit. ("Puppy push-ups," we called these exercises at obedience class.) We would get only two cracks at the ladder that first night and only one try at the plank. Once Willow and I veered too close to the border collie bitch, and I heard a sharp click of teeth closing in the air, a sound like the firing of an unloaded gun. At last it was Willow's turn. He was one of the larger, longer-bodied dogs in the class, and as we approached the plank for the first time, I wondered if he had any notion at all of where his back feet were.

All night Sue had been taking my dog away from me, introducing him to the equipment herself, something she wasn't

16

doing with most of the other handlers. She didn't like my training style, apparently. Remembering that choke collar, no doubt (which I had by now had the belated good sense to remove from around Willow's neck). Then again, we were new to this process. Most of the other handlers, it seemed, had been here before or were already familiar with these new training methods. Still, I had the distinct impression Sue didn't like me. She liked Willow, though. "Such a pretty dog. Very solid disposition. Good drive."

"He doesn't like boards," I warned her. "He got scared on a dock once." When I tugged Willow's leash to position him closer to the plank, Sue took him away from me again.

"Here's how you do it," she said, in an imperious tone. She was showing me, not Willow. I was the slow learner here, not my dog. "Forget obedience class," she said. "No pushing or pulling. Coax him along. Slowly. Gradually. It has to be *his* idea. You are teaching the dog to think." *There's that phrase again.*

Her hands full of treats, Sue led Willow gently to the long board, more by his nose than by the leash. She got him to put up his front paws, supplying a steady stream of encouragement and beef jerky. Willow was gobbling these new and better treats as fast as he could. He started jumping over the board, perhaps confusing it with the jumps we had done in Puppy-K. Suddenly the treats stopped. He eyed Sue curiously, tipping his head. He leaped over the board again excitedly. Again, no treat. He gazed at her, his ears forward, his eyes shining with attention. This was what Sue had been waiting for—for him to try to figure out how to get the treats out of her hand. Willow stared at this odd but sporadically generous human for a moment and then tentatively put a paw on the board. A treat came. Soon Sue had both his front paws up again. There were more treats, and then Sue told me it was time to quit. "That's enough for the first night," she said. "Quit when he does it right. Know when to quit. Did you see that? He's starting to think."

Yes, he was starting to think, I mused, but he was thinking mainly of food. Still, I began to see the genius of the game. The truth was, Willow would probably stand on his head eventually for more of that beef jerky. And what about bacon, I thought, or a little raw tuna? How about some *filet mignon*?

Two

I should probably disclose right now, at the outset, that Willow and I would never become great competitors at dog agility. You will not be seeing us at night on Animal Planet waving to the crowd. While we did have our successes with training along the way, in the end we didn't get far in the sport for reasons that I will go into later. If that's all there was to the story, then it would hardly be worth the paper it was written on. But the experience was, as I have said, really much more than that. Dog agility and the behaviorally based training methods used by agility trainers have, among other things, utterly transformed the way I look at animals, and particularly the four-legged ones who roam the floors of my house. I think that I used to have trouble separating my own needs and desires from those of the family pets. In fact, I used to think of the family pets as extensions of my own needs and desires. If I wanted love, then I would pet the dog. He would wag his tail, and I would think, *Aw, look at that, Fido loves me.* I don't make this mistake anymore.

To show you a little better how I now think of my dogs—I have two of them, though at the time of this agility training I only had the one—I want you to think of space aliens and how they are portrayed on TV and in the movies. Follow me here. This is not an original analogy. It is a comparison that is regularly used by animal trainers, and I think it works. Imagine a space traveler, say on *Star Trek*, say Captain Kirk. On his travels, he encounters an alien from another planet. As he faces this unfamiliar creature, the good captain never automatically assumes that it shares his desires and intentions. In fact, what the alien wants is nearly always the first thing he asks, after counting the number of arms, legs, eyes, and heads. (Of course, beneath the captain's curiosity lies his own burning desire to know, *Is it hungry and does it want to eat me?*) Still, he never assumes he knows what's in the alien's mind. He gazes fixedly at it, fascinated by its every move, until gradually—through its behavior—the alien begins to reveal itself and its purpose.

Now look down, if you would, at the four-legged alien reclining on your living room carpet. (If you don't have a dog, borrow one.) This alien has four knobby paws, a waving tail, wide benign brown eyes, and an eager nose and tongue. A golden? A Lab? A sheltie? What sort of alien creature do you have? Perhaps you are laughing at this point. I know exactly what my dog wants, you say. He wants food, he wants a walk, he wants his butt scratched. But do you? Do you really know what he wants? Remember, this is an alien. Stop assuming things you think you know.

Have you ever really tried to find out what your dog wants or, more importantly, what he'd be willing to do to get it?

Go to the fridge. Take out something really tasty. A chunk of raw beef liver, a hunk of barbequed chicken, that pork medallion out of last night's doggie bag. Now take this prize and go sit on the couch, and watch what your dog will do to get at it. Don't just give it to him. Sit on the sofa and let him figure out how to get it out of your hand. Hold out and watch how clever and inventive he can be. He will start with the old tricks, the ones that have worked for him in the past. Begging, pawing, barking. These are the tricks you have unconsciously taught him by rewarding him with food. Don't reward them this time. Sit and watch while your dog comes up with new things to try. Test his creativity. Pawing, barking, what else? Will he climb up on the coffee table? Will he tug at your pant leg or put his paws up on your chest? Will he risk getting himself in trouble with you? Will he growl, dance on his hind legs, nip your arms? When he gazes at you, wagging his tail and trying to decide what to do next, is he looking at you with adoration (as perhaps you have always assumed), or with abject cunning?

Remember, your dog is an alien. Don't make assumptions.

My guess is that, if the treat is juicy enough and if you hold out long enough, your dog will come up with some truly astonishing efforts to get at this prize. When he does, he will be demonstrating something that nearly all animals seem to be adept at—coming up with creative solutions to get at food. It is something we have all observed in backyard squirrels trying to outfox the latest squirrel-proof feeder—the cagey approaches, the daring leaps. It is this combination of effort and ingenuity that agility trainers are tapping into: What any animal can do when properly motivated by food is rather amazing. Dolphins and other huge marine mammals have been trained to put on daily tank shows for human spectators, a goldfish has been taught to leap from an aquarium, and a pigeon to stand on its wing. You need only, as I did, get over the mental hurdle of wanting to force the animal—in this case, your dog—to do it. Creative and extraordinary performance cannot be forced and will never be obtained through threats and domination. But as I have already noted, old habits die hard.

So it was beginning to work, this teaching the dog to think, although the results were not at first immediately apparent. The night of our second agility class we had nearly given up on the plank. Willow would get his front paws up on the long board and then step back down without ever lifting a rear foot. Sue was working with him again, less to take him away from me this time, than taking him on as a project. Most of the other dogs had already mastered the foot-high plank. Only the two really big dogs in the class, Willow and the Rottweiler, hadn't yet gotten the knack. There were only four dogs in class on this rainy night (Willow's more vicious collie cousins being mercifully absent), and so Sue had the time to try. On his last attempt, Willow finally got a rear leg up on the plank, just one, still standing on the ground with the other foot. Jackpot. Four big chunks of ham and chicken fell from Sue's hand onto the plank. (She had gotten these succulent morsels from the girl with the fat sheltie, and now I knew why he was fat.) Willow slowly chewed this delicious reward and then stepped his three paws daintily back off the board. He sniffed around the ground. Licked Sue's hand. Looked at her. Put up his front paws again. "Yes!" Sue said encouragingly, but no treats this time. She was squatting by the plank now. Waiting him out. Her face was placid. She gazed at Willow, not saying anything. Willow sniffed the plank where the chicken had been. He put his front paws back down on the ground, and sniffed around again. Two long minutes went by, and Sue and I were both ready to give up. (Well, I was.) Suddenly Willow was standing on the plank, all four paws off the ground. Jackpot!

Handfuls of meat fell onto the long board. Big chunks of meat all the way down the plank. I was holding my breath now. Had probably forgotten what breathing was. Willow moved gingerly along the full length of the wooden board, eating all the meat he could find, until he reached the end and hopped off. I greeted him as if he had just saved a drowning child. Sue glared at me, and I didn't understand why. Too much excitement from me, apparently, something that I didn't comprehend at the time. Willow looked merely bewildered at my reaction. *Who wouldn't eat this nice meat?* He was probably thinking. *And why is the boss jumping around like that?*

"I guess all that meat helped," I said, feeling rather giddy, but also somewhat resentful of Sue's success.

Sue gave me one of those perplexed looks that told me I had just said something extraordinarily stupid. "Success in training," she told me, in that preachy instructor's voice of hers, "is directly related to the quality of the treats."

It was the same thing with our next obstacle, the A-frame, which—as its name implied—was an A-shaped configuration of slatted plywood boards that the dogs were to climb up one side of and descend on the other. Willow was reluctant at first, stretching out his long body to reach the treats high up on the ramp, not wanting to let those big haunches of his leave solid earth. Someone had beef liver and lent it to Sue. That did it. Willow crouched low and crept his way slowly up and over the obstacle. "Yes! Yes!" Sue told him. Jackpot. "Watch this dog the second time," she told the class. The second time Willow did not crouch. He breezed over the A-frame standing tall and accepted his liver with a look of entitlement.

So here was the thing: I was slowly beginning to see this dog in a different way. Instead of an unruly puppy jerking at the end of his choke collar, I was beginning to see a thinking, sensate creature who was able to make his own decisions about what he would and would not do. He was not interested in mounting a tall wooden A-frame for commercially produced dog treats. But for beef liver, what the hell, he'd give it a shot. This was what Sue meant when she said that success was largely determined by the quality of the treats. "You're too stingy," she kept telling me. "And you need better treats. Give him a whole handful of meat. Make it worth his while." Finally, I was beginning to catch on. Me. Not the dog. He already knew.

This wasn't dog training, I thought. This was paycheck. This was signing bonus. You want me to mount that obstacle? It's gonna cost you. What's it worth?

Again, I resented it.

This was a dog, not an employee. And I had always bought the whole Albert Payson Terhune line. Weren't collies supposed to perform out of loyalty? Collies were meant to be dedicated, obedient, unquestioning. The good soldiers of the dog world. But he wasn't. Not Willow. He was just as happy to work for Sue as for me. Happier, since she wasn't so sparing with the treats. And usually she had real meat in her hand. So much for canine loyalty. So much for man's best friend.

But it wasn't just that. Not *just* that. There was something more at work here, something else. It was that I was having to treat Willow so much more like—well—like a human. Sue wouldn't let us scold or reprimand the dogs for *not* doing something. In this class, Willow had an absolute right to refuse to do anything he didn't want to do. We could try to convince him that it was in his best interests to mount this plank or that A-frame. But he didn't have to. No one was going to force him.

There was a name for this, I thought. It was called free will. *My god!* I thought. *My dog has free will!* I gazed at Willow in disbelief as he sailed over the A-frame yet again.

The next morning on our usual early walk, Willow was off leash, and my pocket brimmed with ham. We have since moved, but at the time we lived on the muddy banks of a tidal river called the North River less than a mile from where it emptied into the Atlantic. In the mornings, Willow and I would jaunt down the main road, fringed by salt marshes, to a pretty point on the river that was home to several lobster boats. This was a particularly fine morning for September, one of those warm Indian summer days that brings out the bees. A jogger was coming down the road toward us at a distance, also headed out to the point. Willow likes to chase joggers. They are, in fact, his favorite things to chase. Better than cars because they scream and yell when pursued or nipped. Generally Willow doesn't mind coming when called, but he likes joggers better. On this morning, the memory of last night's class was still fresh in both our minds. When the jogger was about a hundred yards away, Willow lifted his head from the bayberry bush he was sniffing and eyed the figure plodding toward us. His body tensed, and he looked at me. Usually, he knew, I would be starting ineffectually to shout, "stay" or "sit" or, preemptively, "bad dog." On this morning, though, instead, I held out a handful of ham chunks. "Willow come," I said in a light, cheerful tone. He trotted over friskily and executed a perfect butt-wiggling sit in front of me, clearly pleased with the knowledge that he had already earned his breakfast. Happily he accepted his reward, and together we watched the jogger trot past. At the time, I remember that this seemed like news to me. Willow had just told me in no uncertain terms that he was willing to forego chasing joggers. Well, maybe. What's it worth?

On some level, this seemed to me quite outrageous. That a dog could have free will. Why was I so flummoxed by this realization? Because I could never imagine that animals might be able to make their own decisions? Because the moment I let Willow exercise his own will he began to seem freer than some people I know? In a way, it was a wonderful thing, liberating. Willow could do anything that I could pay him enough to do. And I could pay him, and pay him well. Ham was cheap. So was beef liver. And I could even sauté it in garlic and butter if he preferred it that way. Yet this understanding made me rather angry. (Angry yet again—who knew what an angry person I was?) Part of me, the controlling part, still wanted to put his choke collar back on him and jerk him till he swore off joggers forever. This part of me still wanted to yank him into next month, into next year, into seeing stars. Here was what was really bothering me: I didn't want to give up the control of *because I said so*. Yet this was exactly what I was going to have to do if we were to accomplish anything at this dog agility training.

On our way back from the point, Willow and I walked together companionably. His tail was carried gaily in the air. He sniffed the bushes and fences we went by, and around the bank of rural delivery mailboxes on our circle. He seemed already noticeably happier with our new relationship. He was a pale golden dog blanched by morning light, his slender, taut body nosing into each smell he found. He looked light, almost weightless with his springy stride, and freer than I could ever recall him looking, though surely it was only my own eyes. As we were nearing home, I remember watching his long nose with its black rubbery tip snuffle a post of the neighbor's split rail fence. This was the post where the neighbor's old cat, CiCi, usually sat and napped in the afternoon sun, and then scratched her claws on a rail. Willow's damp nose investigated the cat's post and then slid down the whole length of the middle rail. As he scented deeply, his eyes slid almost shut. *Look at him,* I mused, *he's thinking. No, he's not thinking. He's dreaming. Dreaming of cats.*

At this point, these new training methods—"positive" training methods, as they are usually dubbed—were beginning to look to me a lot like granting animals a whole new level of freedom, respect, and autonomy that we humans hadn't previously accorded them. But before I get too carried away, and start sounding like a card-carrying member of the animal liberation front, I should say here that, in retrospect, I can clearly see such methods still work mainly to bend animals to our human wills. (One imagines, for example, the dreadful sight of a cow being led happily to its own slaughter on a trail of cow treats.) We are smarter than the animals, which somehow doesn't seem quite fair. Even after having become firmly convinced of the benefits of these new training techniques, it still makes me feel a bit squeamish that we can turn animals' own lusts and desires against them in this way. On the other hand, why should our domesticated beasts be any different from the average American consumer, whose lusts and desires are regularly manipulated through advertising and marketing so that we purchase things we don't really need on our maxed-out credit cards. And these training methods, they are so much more humane than the old ones. How much better it is to see animals lured, encouraged, praised, and rewarded, than it is to see them jerked, choked, pinched, or shocked. But perhaps the most startling thing about these new approaches is how powerful they are. Who would have thought, for example, that an enormous killer whale could be convinced to leap repeatedly through a hoop with no more encouragement than a few fish? Or a rat taught to sniff out land mines for a palmful of Rice Krispies. There is something almost Zen in it: the power of the positive. By working *with* animals rather than *against* them, by harnessing their wills to work in tandem with ours, we thereby increase immeasurably what our respective species can do together. We also make possible a new level of trust and communication that I was only just beginning to appreciate as I really began to work with Willow—with who *he was* and what *he wanted*.

Three

For a long time, the whole concept of "dog training" as we know it today didn't really exist—not at least in the contemporary sense of a standardized set of procedures for convincing a dog to follow human commands that could be used by any handler upon any dog. That is not to say that a pointer was never forced to drop a bird he was holding in his mouth or a border collie coached to move left or right around sheep based upon the pitch of a whistle. Only that until the two world wars, these coordinated tasks seem to have developed much more naturally over time, and more out of the basic nature of the dog and what he was good at, and less out of bending the dog to the human will. With sheepdogs, for example, a dog that was good at stalking and bunching sheep was allowed to breed. A dog that attacked sheep and tore them to pieces was culled. After several generations of this, you had a dog with good crouch, stare, and outrun behaviors whose bite and kill drives were pretty well arrested. A young herding dog would simply be taken to the sheep and allowed to do what came naturally. That is why to this day you will still hear sheepdog people say things like, *A good dog just knows what to do*. Similarly with the protective breeds: Originally a dog probably set up

housekeeping in someone's yard and did what came naturally—
he protected his territory. Eventually dogs that were good at
protection were selected to keep and breed, and the wimps were
culled (which is a nice euphemistic term meaning killed).

Whether this was a desirable state of affairs when compared
with the harsh dog training tactics later employed is a matter open to debate. Certainly for most of our shared dog and
human history, you didn't see much use of choke chains, prong
collars, and ear pinches. On the other hand, a large number
of young animals were probably put to death for little reason
other than that they were the wrong color or nipped the sheep
a bit too hard. My own grandfather is a good example of this
"old school" of behavior management. He was a backcountry
dairy farmer in the Adirondack foothills of Upstate New York,
and he rarely, if ever, spayed or neutered his animals. Puppies
and kittens that weren't wanted or that looked unpromising
were summarily dispatched in a pail of water (a method of
birth control that caused me no end of consternation as a child).
There was no teaching a dog to herd cows. If a shepherding
dog was useful for driving the cows in from the pasture, then
it was kept. If not, well, then you didn't want to know. The
same with my grandfather's beagles. If the dog hunted rabbits
and had a good nose, great. If not, that same dog wouldn't be a
problem much longer, trust me. (We'll get back to my grandfather later.)

This modification of dog behavior mainly through selection
and culling appears to have come to an end sometime around
the Second World War with the movement of large numbers
of people off the farm and into the cities and suburbs. Culling
was a less acceptable practice for family pets than for farm animals, and a growing humane movement introduced spaying

and neutering programs to control the population of unwanted dogs and cats. Along with these changes, during World War II a large number of dogs were required for various duties. Suddenly patrol, tracking, and search and rescue dogs needed to be turned out in large numbers and in a hurry for military service. There was no time for the old, slow breed and cull procedures. Rapid forced training methods were developed and standardized that could basically be used by any handler upon any dog. A large, new cadre of military dog trainers was schooled in these techniques.

Eventually peace returned, and when World War II ended these military dog trainers were discharged *en masse* back into the general populace where they began offering dog training classes to civilian pet owners based upon the military model. In essence, your dog could be drilled like a regular little soldier with choke collar and leash. He could be taught to walk obediently at your heel and to sit, stand, or lie down exactly as if he were a German shepherd marching on a parade ground. It is probably not a coincidence that obedience trials—which the American Kennel Club started fielding back in the thirties— have never quite lost their air of military discipline and soldierly obedience.

With all of these military dog trainers around and needing to make a living, dog training rapidly grew into an industry. By the 1960s and '70s, dog training classes based upon the military model began to be widely offered in communities across the United States. It was to this soldierly type of dog training that I was first exposed as a kid when my mother brought me and my first dog, a small black and white border collie named Tippy, to one of those community dog training classes. There I won a bright scrap of red ribbon and a big load of parental approval at a vulnerable age, ensuring that I would forever afterward be hooked on dogs and dog training.

It was strictly jerk and release choke chain heeling back then, with the standard sit, stay, come, and down obedience commands—and it was exactly this type of forced training that, with few variations, held sway right up through the 1980s and into the early 1990s. In 1986, *The Atlantic* ran a long feature written by Michael Lenehan surveying the dog training methods of the day.[1] There was, of course, Barbara Woodhouse on the TV—the "Julia Child of dog training" as Lenehan calls her—with her cheerful British voice calling "walkies!" and her hard bright jerks on the choke collar. But the foremost authority of the time was Bill Koehler (rhymes with heeler), a compulsion-based dog trainer whose training method, eponymously called *The Koehler Method*, was extolled in a series of well-selling books that advocated a wealth of harsh training tactics.

Koehler was one of those military dog trainers who had begun his career in 1946 at the War Dog Reception & Training Center in San Carlos, California. He later made a successful career out of training movie dogs like Roy Rogers' Bullet and Big Red, the famous fictional Irish setter. Lenehan reported on attending a group dog training session with Bill Koehler's son, Dick Koehler, at the family's compound in Ontario, California, and of seeing not just the jerk and release choke collar training to which my dog Tippy and I had been introduced, but also a number of other harsher tactics, most of which would be considered pretty inhumane by today's standards, but which were widespread at the time. Koehler ran dogs into fence posts to keep them from heeling wide, and clotheslined them by getting the

1. Michael Lenehan, "Four Ways to Walk a Dog," *The Atlantic*, April 1986, v. 257, 35.

dog running in one direction while on a choke collar and leash, and then having the handler rapidly switch directions, thereby "flipping" or "dumping" the dog onto his back—ostensibly so that the dog would "learn to pay closer attention." Recalcitrant or aggressive dogs were shaken by their scruffs, hung by their choke collars, or bludgeoned on the nose with a rubber hose, a technique dubbed by Koehler as "the tranquilizer." Elsewhere in his article, Lenehan describes the use of "throw chains" and shock collars to control off-lead dogs. Although the piece mentions a few trainers beginning to advocate for gentler methods, back then "gentler" seemed to mean using an "escalating" level of violence and resorting to harsher methods only if the softer—but still unkind—ones didn't work. On the whole, it isn't a pretty picture that emerges. Koehler himself ridiculed adherents of kinder training methods as "wincers" and "humaniacs."

To some extent these harsh dog training tactics were justified by the thinking of the day. The prevailing reasoning—inspired by Konrad Lorenz, the founder of the science of ethology—held that your dog was a wolf and that he viewed your family as his pack. On this rationale, it was important to train, dominate, and even punish your dog so that he would know you were the alpha wolf in the pack pecking order and that he wasn't. If the training methods advocated by Koehler and others were perhaps rougher than they needed to be for the average family pet, then that was fine because these tactics reminded your dog that he was the subordinate in his relations with humans. And this, the reasoning went, had to be a good thing.

This was pretty much where things stood right up until the early 1990s when what has been called a "quiet revolution" began to gather momentum. Dog trainers, at least at the higher levels, began turning to more humane training methods that had been developed by dolphin trainers out of the principles of behaviorism. It was a trend which—being dogless for most of the nineties—I have to say I missed. I was now getting a crash course in Sue Reed's beginner dog agility class.

Four

I wish today I could say that after my first two dog training classes with Sue Reed my eyes were opened. That I had seen how much better the positive dog training methods worked than my old harsh tactics, and that my dog was actually capable of participating in his own training, and as a result I immediately had a fit of moral qualms and dispensed with my old ways. This, however, was not the case. Although I never again used a choke collar in Sue Reed's class, because I simply had no choice, I continued to use it on a regular basis whenever I took my dog out for a long walk in the woods—in order to maintain the control I felt I needed over Willow, for he was always pulling and jerking wherever we went. In fairness to my old self, I was dealing with a very large, strong, and vigorous young animal who, it seemed to me, was constantly about to get the upper hand, and this in my own mind justified my regular resort to the chain collar. Whenever we went for a walk at a conservation area—which we did nearly every day—I reasoned that I couldn't very well hold a cookie over his nose the whole way, and I didn't know what else to do. And so there elapsed a period of weeks when I still employed the choke collar on an almost daily basis, in order to keep Willow from yanking my arm the whole time we were out walking. Of course, he did continue to jerk and pull, despite my use of the steel collar—he and his neck soon became accustomed to it. And so we would go the entire way with me ineffectually jerking him by the neck and him occasionally choking and coughing but generally not being deterred from nearly yanking my arm from its socket. At one point during this period, I remember considering consulting a doctor about repetitive strain injury to my right shoulder. Something from agility class must have sunk in, though, and some sympathy must have been leaking into my brain for what was going on inside Willow's head, for there came a day when things did change.

Willow and I were out one morning at World's End, a bucolic oceanside wildlife sanctuary in Hingham, Massachusetts, that affords endless rambles down old, traffic-free country lanes through wide grassy pastures. At one point, a squirrel dashed in front of us, and Willow lunged swiftly after it. Anticipating him hitting the end of his leash, I cranked back on his choke collar, so that I was pulling as hard as I could backward at the same time as he was moving as fast as he could forward. The effect when he did reach the end of his leash must have stunned him, or knocked the wind from him, for although he stayed on his feet, he seemed for a moment to go rather limp. He was spun about by the force I had applied to his neck, so that in an instant he was facing me, swaying, and our eyes met. His eyes had bulged out from the choking, and had blanched white all around the rims. The sight was so hideous and so shocking to me that I immediately dropped the leash, and for a moment we stood like that, the two of us, panting and gazing at each other, the squirrel and our walk utterly forgotten. Perhaps it takes something like that—something stunning—to see what you are really doing. I don't remember our return home or what I did the rest of the day, but that night I do recall having a very vivid dream where I myself was being strangled by a chain around my own neck. In the dream, as the choke collar closed on my windpipe, I remember a shadowy humanoid figure standing over me, and the horrible humiliated feeling of having this figure pull the chain tighter and tighter as I gasped and choked. I awoke, sweating, in darkness, pawing at my neck.

I rose from my bed, still breathing hard, and went downstairs in the dark house—it was two or three in the morning—and began digging under the too-bright kitchen lights through the broom closet. What was I looking for? I'll tell you, because I found them all, and laid them out one by one, loop by loop, on the hardwood floor of the kitchen: The large steel collar that I had used on Willow from eight months old to the present time, when he weighed sixty-five to seventy pounds—a chain loop six inches in diameter gleaming on the oak floor; then the somewhat smaller but still sturdy five-inch loop with its steely glow that I'd used on him from age six months to eight months, when he weighed fifty-five to sixty pounds; then the thinner metal loop that spanned four inches comprehending his fourth to sixth months; and lastly—of course—the one I was really looking for with which to excoriate myself—the little chain link noose that I had used on him from two to four months of age. I laid them all out on the floor in their descending sizes and weights of chain link, but it was this last little circlet, no more than three inches across, that held my eye, glittering under the kitchen's florescent lights. *Had I really used a steel choke collar on a tiny two-month-old puppy? Oh, what was I thinking?*

It was at this point that my husband and Willow, both awake now, came sleepily downstairs to see what was up in the kitchen. My husband Steve, a youthful-looking fifty-year-old trial attorney wearing dark-rimmed glasses and blue gym shorts, stood yawning in the kitchen doorway, gazing at everything that I had pulled out of the broom closet. "Are we cleaning house at three a.m.?" he asked.

"I'm having a crisis of conscience," I said, and pointed to the array of choke collars I had spread out on the floor.

Willow sniffed at them without interest and then went to the door asking to be let out.

"I thought your new trainer didn't want you to use them anymore," Steve said.

"Yes, but I *did* use them."

"Oh, I see," he said, with a grin. "We're having a fit of dog guilt here."

"It's not just that I *used* them," I said. "But that I never really even *thought* about using them. About how poor Willow must have felt."

"So don't use them anymore," he said.

"I'm not kidding, Steve," I said, my voice sounding plaintive in my own ears. "I think someday we'll look back at choke collars the way we now look at the implements of human slavery."

"I think Willow will forgive you," Steve said, "if you take him for a walk." He looked over at the dog, who was still standing by the door. Willow wagged his tail.

"I'm serious," I said, my voice rising with distress.

"I'm not sure what you want me to say," my husband said. He looked over at Willow again. "Here," he said. "I'll take him for a walk." He pulled out the garbage pail from under the sink, scooped up the choke collars, and tossed them in the garbage. "Feel better?" He gathered up the garbage in its plastic trashcan liner and slung it over his shoulder, like Santa Claus with his bag of gifts, and then headed for the door to join Willow—apparently taking the collars to the trash barrels in the shed.

"Can we just throw them out like that?" I called after him. "Don't we have to melt them down or something? Or keep them as evidence?"

Steve paused at the door, his shoulder holding it open for Willow. "You don't want to give them to someone else, do you?" he asked.

I shook my head no.

Without a further word, he went out, following the collie.

A few minutes later, I saw their shadowy forms out our picture windows, walking on the banks of the river in the dark, the silhouetted forms of a man and a dog, side by side. I could see that Steve had his head tilted back, his arms folded, gazing upward. Being a man, he *would* be looking up, I thought, mulling his abstract thoughts, probably looking at the planets and stars. Willow, though, being a dog, had his flat head held low, his long snout buried in the marsh grass, taking in the night smells, the traces of other animals.

The next Tuesday, I stayed after agility class and asked Sue Reed how I could get Willow to walk on leash without pulling. I must have sounded rather desperate, asking this. *Save me from myself*, I seemed to be saying.

"Well, what does *he* want?" Sue asked. Poor Sue. She had still not given up on trying to teach *me* how to think. Lord I was dense. "What does *he* want?" she repeated. When I shrugged and didn't answer, she said, "Move forward. He wants to move forward."

"Okay," I said. "So?"

"So don't let him move forward unless the leash is slack."

"What if he keeps pulling?" I said.

"Just be a dead weight at the other end of the leash," she said. "Wait him out. If the leash isn't loose, no forward motion. Be patient."

The next few days, Willow and I went for a couple of very slow walks indeed, taking a few steps forward each time the leash was loose, and stopping each time he pulled. It didn't take long for Willow to catch on. It seemed like quite a while at the time, but it really was only a matter of a couple hours of "training walking" before he figured it out and took it to heart—once he realized that I was serious, and *we really weren't going anywhere without a loose leash*. I felt pretty foolish when Sue Reed's method worked gently and incredibly effectively— and in a far shorter period of time than all of the months I'd spent uselessly pulling on Willow's various choke collars. I was rather angry with myself for not being able to figure out something so obvious, something so basic. I felt shamed and humiliated. It seemed like such a simple solution. Wasn't I supposed to be a smart person? Why couldn't I figure it out? The whole time I hadn't needed a choke collar at all. There was always a gentler way.

I understand now, there usually is.

II. Communication

Five

Agility is such an odd sport, with all its strange equipment, its A-frames and dogwalks and weave poles, that eventually I couldn't help reading up on where it came from. It turns out that agility originated in 1978 at the huge Crufts Dog Show in the UK—the Westminster Dog Show of England, as most Americans think of it. A member of the Crufts show committee for that year, a man named John Varley, was charged with coming up with the dog equivalent of a Super Bowl half-time performance for the show. Being mainly a horse man, Varley's idea was to create an event that would be like show jumping for horses—only for dogs. Varley enlisted the help of his friend Peter Meanwell, a Working Trials competitor and judge, and the two of them devised a course of jumps and obstacles through which the dogs would race. This demonstration apparently was a huge hit at the 1978 show and was repeated at the 1979 show. In 1980, the English Kennel Club began standardizing dog agility as a sport, setting rules for competition and so forth, and the sport took off—as well it might. It looked like great fast fun to anyone watching it, and could be done (or so the PR went) with almost any dog. And unlike herding, it didn't require a lot of overhead. You didn't need a farm or sheep. Just a large back-yard and some equipment that could easily be constructed out of plywood and PVC tubing from the local hardware store. Soon this new dog steeplechase jumped to Australia, where Varley moved in the 80s, and eventually to the United States, where it met up with the new positive dog training methods just beginning to be touted by writers like Karen Pryor and Gary Wilkes.

The old harsh dog training tactics had held sway right up through the 1980s, but by the early 1990s, dog trainers—at least at the higher levels of competition—were beginning to turn to more gentle training approaches that had been developed based upon the behavioral principles of "positive reinforcement" and "operant conditioning." Around this time, Karen Pryor, who had been a dolphin trainer back in the 1960s and early 1970s, and who helped pioneer these techniques, founded Sunshine Books in order to disseminate information about these kinder animal training methods. Pryor and other "operant" trainers began giving seminars and handing out small handheld "clickers," which were used to "mark for correct behavior" (I'll get to clickers later). The result was that this new training technology suddenly became widely available to dog trainers in the United States for the first time. As with all such thought revolutions, the old guard of military dog trainers came kicking and screaming. The positive techniques couldn't be ignored, though, and for one very simple reason: they worked, and fabulously well. Soon positive trainers were cleaning up in the obedience ring and at agility trials, and having the kind of success that was very hard to argue with.

In her book *Lads Before the Wind: Diary of a Dolphin Trainer,*[2] Karen Pryor described how in the 1960s she and other animal trainers developed these new motivational training methods while teaching porpoises and a variety of other marine mammals to put on shows at Sea Life Park in Hawaii. Although in her book Pryor credits B. F. Skinner and his protégés as the source of these techniques, she perhaps makes a bit much of this connection. She and the other marine mammal trainers were really taking a couple of observations the behaviorists had stumbled upon, and were devising from them a powerful new technological application for teaching skills using food rewards. This wasn't actually a new idea. Certainly there were many historical precursors for training animals with food, most notably in the training of circus animals. But in the world of dog training as it then existed, these ideas were new or revolutionary in the Kuhnian sense of bucking the prevailing trend.

There was a lot of trial and error back in the early days of positive training that is delightfully preserved in Pryor's *Diary of a Dolphin Trainer*—highly recommended reading for anyone who wants to get into animal training. In her book, Pryor related any number of charming tales of creative porpoises and cagey killer whales. Pryor had one big advantage over the other positive trainers—she was a terrific writer. To my mind, she stands in the pantheon of the best science popularizers of our era—as someone who has made sophisticated technical principles simple, available, and understandable to the layman. In the history of dog training, she also stands as the petite girl David who slew the Goliath of the big bad Bill Koehlers of

---

2. Karen Pryor, *Lads Before the Wind: Diary of a Dolphin Trainer,* Revised Edition (Waltham, MA: Sunshine Books, 2004).

the dog training world through a mix of apt theory, cunning application, and the wielding of a sharp pen.

With the publication of *Lads* and *Don't Shoot the Dog!*,[3] Pryor's volume on dog training, the new positive training methods were quickly seized upon by two camps in the dog training community: the service dog trainers and the agility trainers. Why these two sets of dog trainers were so quick to pounce upon these new positive techniques had to do with the needs of their specific fields. In the case of service and guide dog trainers, it was partly an image problem. In the old days, when the harsh tactics held sway, it wasn't uncommon to see a blind person choking, scruff shaking, or even striking his long-suffering seeing eye dog—in those days usually a hollow-eyed, miserable-looking black Lab. Needless to say, this did little to improve the public profile of disabled people, as the service and guide dog trainers were doubtlessly aware, being kind-hearted folks in the helping industry. As soon as something better came along, they—at least many of them—seized on it.

In the case of agility training, the trouble was a little different. The harsher methods simply didn't work. Punitive or "aversive" training tactics—as Pryor will tell you in her books—can sometimes be usefully employed in limited ways to "extinguish" (or eliminate) unwanted behaviors. However, harsh or coercive training methods are next to useless when you are trying to get an animal to perform complex or physically arduous tasks, particularly those that require a lot of handler communication or independent thinking on the animal's part. Punitive or "corrective" methods tend to switch the dog off—off the handler, off the task. This can be a good thing if you

3. Karen Pryor, *Don't Shoot The Dog!*, Revised Edition (New York: Bantam Books, 1999).

are trying to stop a dog from jumping up or biting, but not if
you're trying to get the dog's attention so that he'll work with
you. What rational creature, after all, would want to pay attention to someone who kept pinching his ear? Or play a game
with a handler who insisted upon choking him? As one tracking manual I consulted put it, in cautioning against the use of
harsh training tactics: "I cannot ... envisage anyone teaching
a dog to walk tightropes eight feet above the ground while
carrying a raw egg through compulsion, nor can I picture anyone teaching two aggressive dogs not to fight through induce-
ment." It didn't take agility trainers long to figure out that
they were getting more out of their dogs with the carrot than
with the stick, and now they had Karen Pryor and the other
positive trainers laying out the theory for them, as well as offering sage advice on how to put food rewards on what is called
a "variable reinforcement schedule" (a technique to intensify
behaviors while limiting food rewards) so that they didn't have
to keep stuffing their dogs with treats. A gestalt switch was
underway which, as I have noted, I personally missed.

I should point out here that obedience trainers, with their
long history of forced compliance, and gun dog people, with
their macho hunter's ethic, have been much slower to come
around. It is still, at least on the South Shore of Boston where I
live, quite difficult to find an obedience class at any level that is
really consistent about applying positive dog training methods,
especially for heeling exercises, where choke and prong collars
are still in wide use. And in doing my research for this piece, I
was still able to download from the Web rather explicit instructions from several gun dog and pointing dog sites detailing
how to teach a "forced retrieve" using ear pinches, shock collars,
and "toe hitches." The "toe hitch," according to one source I

consulted, was to be accomplished by positioning the dog on a picnic table and securing a small length of cord to his front leg. The cord was then to be wound around the dog's toes and the trailing end of the cord dropped between the slats of the picnic table. The dog would then be commanded to "Fetch," whereupon the cord was pulled to the point that the dog yelped, or until he took a wooden dowel into his mouth. Knowing what I do now, I find it shocking that such techniques are still in use. The retrieve is truly one of the most straightforward things to teach a dog using positive training methods, especially if a clicker or other marker is employed. Even with my two left thumbs, I have done it, and with a collie who has absolutely no natural retrieving instincts and who abhors holding any foreign object in his mouth—I'll get to that story later. There is really no excuse today for shocking, pinching, or toe hitching that nice doe-eyed pointer or retriever in order to teach it to fetch. Not unless you like inflicting pain on your dog. But then, given the resistance I myself put up in coming over to these kinder training methods, I'm hardly the one to talk now, am I?

Six

I want to back up now and return to our agility training with Sue Reed. By the time Willow and I were a couple of weeks into our training, we seemed to be doing fairly well—or so it appears from the journals I kept to track our training progress. We had by that point gotten to know the other handlers and their dogs, and when we arrived at the big blue equestrian arena, we all wheeled confidently into the muddy parking lot in our vans and SUVs honking hello, the dogs barking at each other through nose-smeared windows. As we climbed out of our vehicles, there was a snap to the air, and dry leaves swirled about our feet, for somewhere along the way it had gotten to be fall. The arena itself, when we entered, was always a hotbed of activity. On any given night, thoroughbred horses were being groomed and tended in stalls that ran along one wall of the building. Inside the arena itself, here would be Sue directing some teenager she had recruited to set up the night's obstacles in a complex pre-set arrangement. While this was going on, there might be an advanced student from another class running his dog—a Doberman or a Belgian Tervuren, perhaps—through a tight series of jumping maneuvers. The place smelled strongly of dog dander and horse manure, and you could always hear a whinny or a stray bark.

Clambering out of our Subaru Outback, Willow seemed like a new dog—now that he had a job to report to and was no longer being punished, at least not in class. Here he knew what was coming and the range of tasks he was likely to be asked to perform, and his movements had taken on a brisk, almost professional air. He entered the arena tail up, his neck arched beneath his big collie ruff, poised for whatever would come next. He strode about the sawdust floor with the disciplined focus of an engineer at a car factory, reviewing the obstacles that had been erected and checking for any changes from last week. (Was the plank set higher or lower? Had the jumps been moved? Did the tunnels smell differently?) He greeted the other dogs with a friendly interest, yet with a new reserve, no longer going to pieces when he saw them. Utterly gone was the crazed puppy I used to know. My goodness, I thought, what had happened to this young dog? My big task with him now was in making sure he didn't burn himself out with anticipation before we ever got to class.

Watching Willow move about the arena with his new businesslike air, I remember being fascinated and somewhat amused by his liking to have a job—by this dog going to work with a lunch pail in hand. I think now that dogs, and, yes, people too, like to be asked to do things—to do tasks, and to be rewarded for doing them. On our own, we are all a bit lazy, are we not? (How hard it was for me to sit down this morning and write!) But applying ourselves to something gives us a good feeling, a sense of satisfaction and accomplishment—feelings that are reinforced by our reward at the end of the day or week, whether it be the money we receive, or—in the dog's case—meat and praise—bonuses that are all the more satisfying for having been earned.

From my observations of Willow, I don't think these feelings are all that different for a dog than they are for a human being. Dogs—at least working dogs—seem to like being asked to perform, and being paid for doing so. In retrospect, I think we do many of the dogs in our care a real disservice by allowing them to become indolent, spoiled members of our households, idle creatures who need do nothing other than eat and sleep and, on occasion, walk. Surely this is a state into which many of us would lapse if permitted to do so, but who would be happy that way? In my experience, what makes a dog's eyes shine, what lifts his tail and fluffs his coat, is—as is often the case for us—competence.

So what was it that Willow was developing competence at? Here was what we had learned by the middle weeks of the semester:

We had learned to whip through several varieties of long curving tunnels—some of them colored a scary black inside to block out the light, some made partially of a soft fabric that collapsed on the dogs as they ran through. We had learned to fly over a series of low bar jumps set either in straight lines or in easy curves, and to bounce a bit higher through a doughnut-like "tire" jump. (Willow was too young to jump very high, and so for now all his jumps had to stay quite low.) We had mastered stepping through the ladder on the ground and walking along the low plank. We had learned to hop up on a square table called a "pause box" where the dogs were required to sit or lie down for a few moments before jumping off. And we had, of course, nailed that A-frame—Willow continued to love this obstacle. He liked being way up in the air like that, King of the Hill, and sometimes couldn't resist stopping up there to admire the high view. (Perched up on the apex of the A-frame, he looked for all the world like a Lassie-colored mountain goat.) Sue was now starting to introduce us to the weave poles, something she seemed in no real rush to do. At the moment, the poles were arranged in two straight lines, so the dogs needed only to run down the middle between them. Eventually the two lines of poles would be squeezed tighter together so that the dogs would have to begin bending and weaving their bodies around the individual poles.

As we mastered these various obstacles, Sue also started combining them in sequence, so that we might do a series like this: jump, jump, tunnel, box. Or, jump, jump, A-frame, tunnel. The dogs really seemed to enjoy these drills. Once they had learned the individual obstacles, it was great fun to race or whoosh through a few of them at a time. Things would begin to get hard again when we started asking them to discriminate among several obstacles, or to choose to perform a hard obstacle when it was stationed next to an easy one, but for the moment the obstacles were all easy, and they were lined up in a row, and it was all fast, fast fun—with treats and big praise at the end, of course.

When I said that "we" had learned these tasks, what I actually meant to say was that these were the tasks the *dogs* had mastered. We *humans* were learning other, less glamorous and more rudimentary things. Like not stepping on our dogs' paws when we were running alongside them. Like not tripping over our own two feet while calling out the requisite commands and at the same time trying to wrestle a treat from a pocket or treat bag. Like not getting tangled up in the leash, which might or might not still be attached to the dog, depending upon the exercise.

Agility training, it turns out, requires far more timing and coordination than the average human being possesses. Certainly more than I possess. I have always found the task of running an agility course with my dog while calling out the names of the obstacles very much like trying to rub my head and pat my belly simultaneously. Add to these tasks a stray leash and a treat bag from which treats must be extracted at just the right moment, and I am lost. Timing, it turns out, is extremely important in agility training. The dog must be presented with the treat at just the right moment, just when he has, say, emerged from the tunnel, when it will be a reward for performing the obstacle, and not a few seconds later when the same treat will be merely a snack. Sue would not let us run with treats in our hands since this would be too distracting for the dogs, who would then be paying attention to the food and not to their handlers' voices or to what they were supposed to be doing. She didn't want a dog falling off the high A-frame because he was busy eyeing that piece of steak in your hand. This meant that the treat had to be pulled from the handler's pocket at just the right moment and swiftly delivered in front of the dog's nose. At this graceful ballet of concerted movements, I was proving an inordinate klutz.

I recall vividly one evening stepping up with Willow to a series of three low bar jumps in a row ending with a tunnel. The third jump, I should add, was a "wing" jump, with triangles of wood appended to either side and sticking out about eight inches. We took off. I remember shouting "jump" twice to Willow, and then reaching the third jump and realizing that after this jump I was going to need to shout "tunnel." (Also I was probably already worrying about wrestling that treat from my pocket.) Suddenly—under the pressure of the moment—I couldn't remember the name for that long tubelike accordion thing that I was supposed to be naming for my dog. Distracted by trying to recall the right word for tunnel, I caught my left sneaker on the wing jump just as Willow cleared it and fell down quite spectacularly in a dark nimbus cloud of sawdust, unhurt but pretty embarrassed. Willow, who was ahead of me, kept going and entered the tunnel as he was supposed to do. When he came out the other end (which was right near my head since the tunnel was curved in a semicircle), he came nosing over as if to say, "Hey, what happened to you, boss?" I had the momentary good sense to roll over and pull a treat from my pocket, and feed it to him right there, lying on my back. It wasn't his fault I fell down. He did everything right. I was the one who messed up.

Actually, it seemed like I was usually the one who messed up, not the dog. I was the one who forgot to shout the names of the obstacles ahead of time as I was supposed to do, or who tripped over the collie, or failed to deliver a treat to him in a timely fashion. And of course, there was always a good audience for your clumsiness, all those pro and semipro dog people lined up behind you waiting to run their own drills. When you pulled a stunt like this, they would gaze sideways at you and edge away from you a little, apparently not wanting to be associated with such incompetence. In Sue Reed's class, there was none of the usual good humor about mistakes that you would normally expect to find in a beginners class. And then there was Sue herself. She had warmed to me noticeably by this time, now that I had come around to her positive training methods, but she remained throughout the course a demanding teacher who let you know at every turn that she expected a high level of performance. She did not find beginner screwups the least bit amusing, and she let you know it.

Fortunately there were other humans who pulled stunts nearly as spectacular as my own, saving me the added humiliation of being *the only one*. I saw a woman trip backwards over a jump she was trying to coax her dog over, and land in a sitting position, swearing. One evening a man clobbered his head loudly on the A-frame as he was running past, drawing blood. In this and the other beginner level agility classes we would take, the handlers—especially the newer handlers—were always hurting themselves or tripping over their own feet or doing weird, uncoordinated things. They would shout directions to their dogs too late or not at all, or call "A-frame" when they really meant "tunnel" or "jump." The poor, poor dogs, I would think to myself. I would imagine them clustered together after class comparing notes. *Did you see what my stupid human did? Oh, no, mine was much worse!*

The dogs were never as uncoordinated or foolish as their people, and I sometimes wondered why that was. Animals seem to have more natural dignity and grace than we humans do. Perhaps this is because they are less self-conscious or less abstract in their thinking. They must find us quite pathetic to watch, as we try and correct ourselves midstride only to trip and fall down in front of them. Replaying in my head the silliness of my own handling, at least early on, I am put in mind of some heavy flightless fowl attempting to fly. I would flap my wings as hard as I could, become airborne for the briefest moment, and then come crashing back to earth. There was that moment, though, when you were up in the air, before you fell, when you were floating and it felt really good. You were working together with your dog for the first time. You were a team, the two of you. Lassie and Timmy. You were a new kind of pals, and you could do great things together. You were colleagues digging into the work side by side, and it was a blast.

Willow felt it too. I could see that he did—from the way he held himself as we approached each new set of obstacles. I could see him craning forward, increasing his attention and focus. His ears would be set cupped open, his nostrils flared. There was a slight loft to the white fur at the base of his neck. He would dive ahead with an acute interest. And with each class—as he gained familiarity with the equipment and confidence in the drills—he improved in his speed and sureness. He also began watching my own body much more closely, attending to any subtle shift in the set of my shoulders or the tilt of my spine indicating which obstacle would be next, or signaling a change of direction or speed. Often he had picked up on where we were going or which obstacle would be next long before I ever got around to announcing its name, something that at first mystified me. *How did he know where we were going before I told him?*

Much of dog communication, it turns out, is nonverbal, and dogs seem vastly to prefer physical cues to spoken ones. Willow was literally *reading my body* as we worked, a process that at first felt extremely odd to me and rather uncanny, but that soon felt wonderful, for it was his keen attention to what I was doing— in those brief airborne moments at the beginning—that was starting to make us feel like a team. And moving beside me in this way, he exuded such lively energy and verve. His long face was bright and eager; his tail waved gaily. He was rapidly becoming what in dog training parlance is called a "happy working dog." He was working with me, and was happy, calm, and confident about doing so.

It was interesting for me to contrast this new "happy dog" attitude with Willow's old mental state under the regime of forced work to which he had previously been subjected. Before starting our agility training, Willow and I had done weeks and weeks of obedience training where he was constantly threatened with discipline (those choke collars and my old scruff shake). He was working—heeling or whatever—under orders and fear of punishment. The work was not done happily and willingly, but under pressure and because he saw no other choice. That certainly was how he looked when I had the choke collar on him. He would stand or walk slowly, his head held low and balky, avoiding eye contact with me or giving me quick nervous glances. That, or he would be out of control, barking crazily and lunging, or trying to run away.

It was as if by trying to control Willow too tightly, by setting the strictures upon him too rigidly, I was inviting him to resist or rebel against my authority. And now in this agility class, once I had loosened the binds upon him and given him tasks he knew he could do and for which he would be rewarded, it was as if I had given him permission to work happily with and for me, rather than against me. His only frustration now was that I often didn't work quickly enough, or in the way he wanted me to. At times, he would nip my rump to drive me toward the A-frame or the tunnel so that he could earn a treat on one of his favorite obstacles. He didn't like it when we had to stand in line in class. *Let's move it*, he seemed to say. *What's the hold up here?* He would bump me with his shoulder to get me moving in the right direction, yip at me, nuzzle my treat pocket.

With each brief class, he seemed to make enormous gains, not only in attention and confidence, but also in self-control and—above all—in calmness. *In calmness.* This was my other observation of him. That he was a noticeably calmer dog than he was just a few classes before. I remember marveling at how quickly Sue Reed was able to transform my crazed, lunging puppy into a focused canine student, working for treats. Early on, though, I think that I thought it was merely a fluke, or perhaps Sue had some kind of animal trainer's magic powder that she was sprinkling on his nose or something. Looking back on it, though, what is truly amazing to me is the speed with which this alteration in my young dog took place. It wasn't an overnight thing at all, but rather was a profound and permanent change in Willow's personality that became more and more evident with each class we attended, so that, by the time several classes had gone by, he seemed a very different dog. He was no longer all over the place. He seemed to have gotten hold of his young body. He moved about smoothly and sleekly and with a new sense of mission. He watched me owlishly for signals radiating from my face or shoulders, or came over and nosed my hands, or gazed inquiringly in my eyes. *What's next?* He had never looked at me in quite this way before, and the warm intensity of his eyes made my heart beat a little faster.

Now I will grant you that collies are one of the more tractable breeds of dog, and that a certain degree of what dog trainers call "biddability" (or willingness to take direction) is hardwired into these animals. Still, who knew what a difference having a job could make? These days whenever I see someone manhandling an especially unruly dog, or see a dog throwing itself gasping and choking at the end of its leash, or crashing against someone's storm door, I no longer think, *It's too bad that poor person got stuck with such an out-of-control animal.* Or, *I wish someone would shut that dog up.* Instead I think, *That dog needs a job.*

I think now that assigned tasks are extremely soothing for dogs. A job gives you something to focus your mind upon and turn your attention over to, so that you are no longer at loose ends. Dogs are such physical creatures that being at loose ends means, for them, being out of control and crazy: they bark, jump, throw themselves around. They launch themselves at doors, knock people over, even growl and bite. (Who has not experienced dogs like this? Who does not have friends with dogs like this?) In my experience, these unwanted behaviors seem to evaporate almost magically once something focuses the dog's attention, and specifically when the dog has some assignment that he wants or needs to do.

Dogs are well able to control their behavior, as anyone can attest who has ever watched a dog sneaking up on a cat or a squirrel. Not a single stray hair moves as the dog oozes along the ground in slow motion, placing one paw stealthily ahead of the next—until the exact moment when he knows that he will pounce. Yes, dogs can assert control over themselves. Certainly they can. But they have to *want* to do it—they have to be *motivated*.

The thing you most notice about well-trained dogs is how much calmer and more pleasant they are to be around than other dogs. They tend not to jump or throw their bodies at you, but greet you with a greater reserve. Even if they are waiting around with nothing to do, they often have been taught more desirable behaviors to resort to rather than jumping, barking, or biting. They sit and ask sweetly for a cookie, or offer you a paw. They bring you a stick or a ball, or drag over the leash. These are dogs who have control over their own behavior. They are also used to communicating with humans, and to being listened to.

I sometimes wonder now why people don't develop more communicative relationships with their dogs. I can understand that few will want to undergo the kind of rigorous formal training that Willow and I did—for one thing, it's too time-consuming. But dog owners should at least get used to the idea of *listening* to their dogs, and to rewarding good behavior. I have come to believe that much of the trouble is that dogs do not speak, at least not verbally, and that, in order to communicate with a dog, you need to be willing to attend closely to his body language, because—except for the occasional bark or whine—most of his language will be physical. I think we humans are such good verbal speakers that we become lazy and expect that this is the only way to communicate—by shouting commands—and that we tend to underestimate or ignore the nonverbal ways in which our animals speak to us.

That certainly was how I used to be. I think we humans are unobservant and therefore bad at body language, and that we need to learn to attend better to what the animals in our care are telling us, and to let them know back—by rewarding the good things they do—what we want from them. When dogs lunge and bark and throw themselves around, that is the equivalent in human terms of shouting for attention. When a dog knows that he's communicating, he no longer needs to yell.

At this point in our agility training, I'm not sure how much of this I yet understood. I'm not even quite sure I saw what was happening to Willow and me, and that we were communicating much better and doing it through nonverbal cues and rewards. But I *could* see the huge change in my dog. I felt thrilled and somewhat mystified by the seeming magic of this positive training. By how it had calmed and focused my yearling collie, and had seemingly wiped away the nervous, unruly, and distracted side of him that used to be so much a part of what I had to deal with when I was around him. I can't say that Willow became a perfect dog overnight, or that he never again had another barking fit or exhibited frustration. But the change I saw in him was both rapid and startling. I began to feel a slow, creeping pride in him—in this new Willow. With this level of drive, focus, and control, it seemed that the possibilities were boundless. Together there was nothing we couldn't do. Indeed, at this point, *I* seemed like the one destined to hold *him* back, with my two left feet and my complete inability to do two things at once.

At that moment, I think I fell a bit in love with this dog. I romanticized Willow the way you might a lover. When love is new, anything is possible, and your fantasies can run riot. I dreamed of the two of us winning brightly colored ribbons. Or of standing on top of one of those three-tiered podiums, raising high a tall trophy—the kind my son once bought home from a karate tournament—except that, instead of a kicking boy on top, this one had a silver collie leaping through a hoop. I fantasized about us going to the Agility Olympics (whatever that would be—I had, at this point, only the vaguest notion of what an agility competition even looked like, never actually having been to one before). This was a magical moment at the beginning, when things were clicking and there were no limits. My sense of possibility and optimism wiped away any remaining vestiges of the original resentments I may have felt about having to bribe and reward my dog, and made of me a complete and total convert to these new positive dog training methods. It is ironic (if perhaps inevitable) that this would happen at the very moment Willow and I were about to hit our first real training snag.

I should note here that I surprised myself, developing ambitions for this sport. I had started agility training almost as a lark. It had been a long time since I'd done any serious dog training, really since the 1980s when my last collie, Pooh, was a youngster. At first, agility had just seemed like something fun to do with the family dog. Now here I was, suddenly getting caught up in this new dog sport. And maybe that's all it was—getting caught up in a sport. It's easy, when you are taking weekly lessons in something, to have that activity start to take on a disproportionate importance in your life, whether it be golf, or tennis, or dog training. But I think there was something else going on, too—something that perhaps I didn't fully appreciate at the time. I think that, having won that little red ribbon all those years ago with my dog Tippy, I had lurking within me the desire to do it again—to bring home ribbons. I had never done any competitive dog training since that time. And though I had always trained my dogs, I had done so only to make them behave better, and to provide myself with more pleasant and tractable pets, and not to win any prizes. But I believe now that the desire was still there. And all it took was for Willow to look the least bit promising for the briefest period to bring those old ambitions to the surface.

Seven

As with giving up force, learning to really attend and listen to my dog's physical language took some time to sink in. In class, I had learned to pay closer attention to Willow and what he was doing—and he to me—but I have to say that it took a number of weeks before I really began applying what I had learned *outside* of class, at least consciously. There did, however, come a brilliant November day—as Willow and I were out walking at a remote nature area amongst orange and yellow foliage lit by bright sunlight—when things seemed suddenly to click.

Because we were way out in the woods with nobody else around, I wasn't concerned about Willow taking off to go explore someone's yard, or about him running off with another dog, and so I let him off leash to dash in and out of the brush looking for small animals. There was an avalanche of acorns that year, bringing with it an excess of small red ground squirrels. Willow flashed madly about, looking lovely with the sun glinting off his golden coat, set off by the red pine needles underfoot and the blazing foliage and blue sky overhead. With the strong scent of rodent in his nose, he took to racing ahead on the twisting path. I would find him waiting for me at each divide in the trail, his face bright and attentive—just as in class—waiting for me to tell him whether to go right or left where the trail split. At first I would shout "left" or "that way" and swing my arm the way I wanted him to go, and he, accustomed by now to taking such direction from me, would bolt down the correct trail and wait for me at the next trail junction.

After a few such junctions—and there were many because this was a twisty nature path with lots of intersecting trails—I found that I could completely dispense with all verbal commands. As in our agility class, Willow wasn't listing to what I was *saying*, he was looking at my *body*—at the tilt of my head and the set of my spine. I had only to dip my head ever so slightly in the direction I wanted him to go, and off he would speed the way I had indicated. How lovely this was for me, this silent communication. Wordlessly we made our way along for over an hour, with a mere nod of my head or a flip of my hand telling my dog where we were going, and with him bolting off and then flashing back for more subtle, wordless communication—heart-stoppingly gorgeous in his blond coat and white feathers—the only sounds those of my own breathing and my boots hollow on the soft earth, occasionally breaking a stick or crunching leaves.

Now that I had fallen silent and was attending better to Willow, I found that I had the uncanny experience of benefitting more from his own superior senses, his keener nose and his finely-tuned hearing. If I watched him closely, I could detect small animals that I would never have found on my own. If I followed his long nose as it explored the ground, I could make out the paths those same animals had trod, confirmed by broken sticks and tamped down undergrowth that would have been invisible to me, if not for my dog. Dogs are nothing if not geniuses of the senses. They can pick up the faintest traces of scent on the trail or wind, or hear a stick breaking or a quiet bark half a mile off. And when we are with them—we can extend our own senses merely by attending to them. It felt to me that day as if the woods had opened up to reveal some of its secrets. As if my own senses had thrust deeper into the mysteries of the forest, thanks to my alert collie. I felt acutely sensitive myself. It was as if my own sensory world had enlarged. Since that day, long trail walks in the woods with my dog (now dogs) have become one of my favorite things to do. I never fail to take pleasure in the expansion of my senses, and in the silent, subtle communication that is possible between human and canine out in the natural world.

III. Skills

Eight

Once we agility students—human and canine—had begun settling into our training, this was the moment when Sue Reed began raising the bar. With each new class, each piece of apparatus got a little harder or higher. The jumps, for instance, until now had been set at about six to eight inches high—pretty low considering that a dog Willow's size would eventually have to jump twenty-four inches on a standard agility course. The jumps in class now rose to around a foot high. The tunnels, too, got harder. Sue sharpened the bend at the middle of the dark tunnel so that the dogs couldn't see any light coming in from the other end as they entered. Also, she had been holding open the soft fabric of the collapsing tunnel (or "chute") so that the dogs could see where they were going, but she now began dropping the soft, floppy material on their heads and shoulders so that they had to push blindly through to the end. The A-frame was noticeably higher and steeper. The two lines of weave poles had squeezed tighter together. There were sharper turns in the sequences of obstacles we were running. All of these challenges Willow met and conquered without difficulty—so long as I kept some sufficiently delectable reward ready at my hip.

I should say something here about the treats I was now offering Willow in agility class. Sue had by this time convinced me that new and better training rewards were key in getting our dogs to tackle these harder challenges and in keeping them working happily. Given the enormous changes I was seeing in Willow (and my own growing ambitions), I was fully prepared to go with this idea. Now that the obstacles were becoming more difficult, I determined to provide Willow with something considerably better than the commercially produced dog treats I had previously bought for him in the pet food aisle of the grocery store. Sue told us to go online, where we could find recipes for making really good dog cookies. That, or go to the grocery and buy meat that could be cooked and cut up into bite-sized chunks for class. I decided to opt for the latter course—even though most of the time my husband and I are largely vegetarian—since what Willow really seemed to want was meat, real meat.

Why would a vegetarian cook meat for her dog? I think there was a mission I was on that was not yet fully clarified in my consciousness—a desire or a wish to meet Willow on his own terms. As I have said, I no longer saw him as a dumb puppy jerking at the end of his leash. Rather, I had begun to view him as an intelligent creature who could make his own decisions and who had decided to work happily with and for me. He was giving me what I wanted, and I, in turn, wished to give him what it was he wanted. I remember thinking at the time that, for a dog, agility training must tap into a very basic instinct—that of hunting. The dog was being asked to pull off complex and demanding maneuvers at the instruction of his handler in order to get at fresh dripping meat. How could this not tap into some very primitive urges Willow must have received from his wolfish forebears—to perform coordinated and moderately dangerous activities for food? This must all be very exciting for him, I thought. No wonder he loves this training so much. No wonder he's working so enthusiastically. And so I decided that I would satisfy his desires, his wish to hunt. I would buy him *real* meat to reward him with. If I was going to ask him to do these difficult and rather risky things, it seemed like the least I could do.

This task, though—of buying and cooking Willow real meat—was not without its own absurdities. A day or two before agility class, I would go to the local grocery stores looking for the boneless chicken that was on sale according to the circulars, or for the cheaper cuts of steak being advertised. But as I browsed the meat coolers at Stop & Shop or Shaw's, I would invariably, it seemed, find myself standing next to some stooped elderly lady with peach-colored hair, or a young person in worn-looking footwear and jeans, who apparently was shopping for the same inexpensive cuts of meat as me, but for a very different reason. I always felt a stab of remorse as I scrutinized the White Hen chicken breasts nearing their freshness dates or the fatty, grisly hunks of chuck steak. So many people in the world could barely afford enough wheat or rice to fend off starvation, and here I was buying steak for my dog.

This, of course, did not deter me. I would snatch up my prizes and—casting a guilty glance at the person standing next to me—beat a hasty path for the checkout, my head and shoulders curled in upon themselves, my expression that of a thief. In the checkout line, I was likely to encounter a stray comment—from someone standing ahead of or behind me in line—who, appraising all the meat heaped in my shopping cart, would toss off some remark to the effect of, "I'd like to come to *your* house for dinner," or "If you're making those chops, I'll be over at six." We won't even broach the subject of all those dead mammals and fowl whose glistening body parts lay bloody and Saran-wrapped back in the meat cooler. So much for my high-minded ideals about communicating with animals. So much for viewing them as sensate beings.

The real irony here is that my husband and I rarely eat meat, in no small part out of our moral qualms about doing so. At the time of this training, we had both recently read Peter Singer's landmark 1975 work, *Animal Liberation*, and we were well acquainted with the cruelties inflicted upon animals by the agricultural food production industry in this country—the inhumane feedlots, the horrors of the slaughterhouse. We had both had our moments of queasiness at the grocery store as we surveyed the cases of red meats displayed upon their soggy pink beds of waxed cotton and Styrofoam—a sight that smacked to us more of the morgue than of food. Most days we dined (and still do) mainly upon dishes made with rice, pasta and vegetables flavored with a few unfortunate shrimps. My dog, however, had no such scruples about eating other animals and was an unregenerate carnivore. And I found myself in the un-savory role of his procurer. Leaving the grocery store carrying his training meat, I always felt a bit like a supplier for a crack addict.

At home things were little better.

When you are almost exclusively vegetarian, it is a mouth-watering event to enter your small galley kitchen to find a large hunk of red meat sizzling in a skillet dressed only with a dash of salt and a squeeze of zest from the garlic press. Imag-ine, then, the first few times I cooked these dog delicacies and my husband, Steve, came poking hungrily into the kitchen in his jeans and bare feet, a befuddled expression on his face. He sniffed the rich, burnt air, redolent of grease and heated flesh, and said in a tone of complete bewilderment something like, "Is this for *us?*" or "Are you cooking *this* for dinner?" "Out," I told him and elbowed him away from the hissing, spitting pan. "It's for the dog." He gazed at me in mock horror and said, "For the dog," like that—a statement—then shook his head and exited the kitchen, leaving behind him a few mournful mooing noises.

Actually, my husband seemed both amused and somewhat offended by this extravagance in the name of dog training. Not only is he a vegetarian; he is also from a parsimonious Yankee family. And I think that, in his view, that squeeze of garlic zest for added flavor probably lay somewhere on the margins of good sense and sanity. But then, he likely understood that I was caught up in the throes of this new passion—this dog agility training. He knows that I quickly lose my powers of rational cogitation when I am caught in the thrall of some such passionate pursuit—usually something I am writing about—and I suspect that he rather loves me for it. We are still married as of this writing, though after all of the meat I have by now cooked for the dog and not for him, I suspect that I'm on permanent probation with the caveman side of him.

When the meat was seared outside, but still red and bloody in the middle, I transferred it to the cutting board and let it cool. I then sliced it into bite-sized chunks, and it was these yummy morsels that I now pulled from my treat bag in agility class. Yes, I bought a treat bag. Even cooled, the meat was too messy to put in my pocket. So I went online and purchased from an agility website a special treat-holding bag that clipped to my belt. As with every other specialized area of human endeavor, agility has developed its own complex social and cultural structures on the Internet. And so I found agility websites and websites for agility magazines and agility subscriber lists. There was agility advice for the newbie, and there were agility forums where instructors could spend a lot of time crabbing about having to teach those very same newbies. The website I visited was ancillary to a print magazine called *Clean Run* (a "clean run" being when you complete an agility course with no faults or knocked bars.) *Clean Run's* website listed upcoming agility trials and events. It also offered a line of agility books and products, as well as links to other vendors and resources, and this was how I purchased my treat-holding bag—a small, doubled-lined green pouch with a drawstring neck made of the same material as backpacks.

While shopping for my treat bag, I also considered ordering an agility T-shirt (there were some really cute ones, mostly making fun of border collies and how smart they are); something called a "clicker" that I seemed (according to the websites) to require—I had at this point seen a few other students using these small handheld devices in class, but I didn't yet understand what they were for; and my own dog jump for home so that Willow and I could practice between classes. I decided to hold off on these purchases, though, until my husband recovered from the shock of all the meat I was buying, and until I could ask Sue Reed what a clicker was and if I really needed one. For now Sue would tell me that I didn't require one. I should be able to "mark" Willow's correct behavior using just my voice, she said—by saying a sharp, staccato *"Good!"* or *"Yes!"* at the exact moment when he did something right, and then immediately rewarding him. It would only be later that I would come to appreciate what a powerful communication tool a clicker could be—a sort of Morse code for speaking to my dog—but that was still a ways off. And so I ended up with just the treat bag, and it was this cute little number riding on my hip out of which I now fished Willow's chunks of chicken and garlic-sautéed steak at agility class.

One evening Sue tilted the end of the plank up against the pause box. Remember the plank? That twelve-foot hunk of wood that in the first class had given Willow and me so much trouble? Until now, it had lain comfortably parallel with the earth and a mere nine or ten inches high. Willow had mastered walking on it those first two classes and had done so with apparent ease for several weeks. Now, though, things were about to get harder again. On this particular night, a plank fitting the same description was dug into the sawdust at one end and leaned up against the twenty-inch high pause table (or "box") at the other end. The dogs would be asked to climb up this narrow ramp to the box, where they would receive a treat and then hop off. They were used to getting treats up on the box from the short sequences we had been running, which often ended there, and so there was a real incentive to get up there, as well as the force of habit carrying them up. What Sue was doing was getting us ready for the big "dogwalk"—the balance beam for dogs—which would consist of one twelve-foot plank rising to a height of about four or five feet, then another twelve-foot plank running across the supports in a sort of narrow bridge at this height, and then finally another plank of the same length descending at the other end. What we were seeing here was the upslope of the dogwalk. Once the dogs had mastered the climb up this narrow slope, Sue would bring out the real thing—the big dogwalk—for us to try.

Willow and I stood in line, waiting our turn at this new piece of apparatus. (I was hanging back a bit because of our previous plank troubles.) As we waited, I examined the inclined plank and felt myself begin to worry. The plank looked rather steep and narrow to me. It was, as I have noted, only twelve feet long and rose nearly two feet over that distance, which at the time seemed like a lot to me. I tried to relax and hoped that I was not communicating my own apprehension to my ever-vigilant collie. We watched the other dogs try it. The shelties, of course, popped right up the narrow slope, as did most of the other canine students. As before, only the big Rottweiler seemed to have trouble. He walked his front feet up the incline but tried to leave his back feet on the ground as his front feet walked higher and higher. Eventually he jumped off without reaching the pause table.

At last it was Willow's turn, and I braced myself for what I was sure was coming, but my dog had no such difficulties. Twice he walked calmly up the steep, narrow slope and received his treat, and then stood placidly on the pause box, chewing it. It was as if his confidence had carried him up. He had been on a winning streak and (unlike me, apparently) expected nothing untoward to happen.

Then, suddenly, something *did* happen. To this day, I still don't know for sure what it was (though I now have my theories).

Although Willow had already twice ascended the plank without a hitch, now suddenly—and for no apparent reason—he refused to mount the plank and then the pause box—which is to say that his refusal began with the inclined plank and then, later on in the class, extended itself to the box.

When this first happened, it caught me by surprise. Willow had been trotting up the plank so happily that I simply wasn't expecting it. And yet suddenly he wouldn't go near the plank, no matter how nicely I asked or what tasty treat I pulled from my treat bag. What had happened, I wondered. Did he stub his toe? Twist an ankle? (He looked as if he might be limping a little.) Did he catch a splinter from the rough wood surface in one of his paw pads? I checked his feet carefully and found nothing. If there was limping at all, it seemed to have gone away, leaving me uncertain that it was ever there in the first place.

The class progressed. Soon the smaller dogs were all pouncing happily upon the inclined plank and climbing to the pause box—the shelties, the smaller border collie (the larger, snappier bitch by now having dropped out of class), the springer spaniel, even the low-slung basset. When the plank was tilted upward, the smaller dogs seemed to like it even better than when it was level, and they hopped upon it almost gleefully, dancing up the full length, gobbling treats. They jockeyed for their place in line so that they might be next.

Poor Willow. He saw the other dogs and knew that he was the dunce. He made a few halfhearted runs at the bottom of the steep plank, each time turning away from it at the last moment. His ears and tail sagged. He barked with frustration, nipped at my treat bag containing the new tastier dog treats that he was no longer getting, and tugged toward the A-frame where he knew that he could still be a star and wanted to show off. The Rottie was doing a little better than Willow. He at least wasn't trying to avoid the plank altogether. Both of the big dogs, though, refused to put their rear legs up on the inclined board, and so Sue sent them back for more work, back to the first plank we had trained on—the level plank, still parallel with the earth and less than a foot high.

At first, Willow wouldn't approach even this low plank, level or not. The Rottie put his front paws up on it and cocked his ears at his handler and at Sue. *How's this?* he seemed to ask, in his doggie way. His brow wrinkled like an old man's. Oh, god, I thought. Isn't this exactly where we were back in the first class? Soon Willow was pulling the same old tricks as he had before. He jumped over the plank, or edged along it with his front feet, hoping that we would be happy with anything short of a full rear-end mount.

Sue worked repeatedly with both dogs, with both Willow and the Rottie. At last she got the Rottie's back paws up on the plank, albeit briefly. But not Willow's. It seemed to me as if we were back to square one. Back to before square one. Sue called Willow a "poop." "No more treats for you, you poop," she said. "Not until both feet are up." (She had been rewarding him for a single back foot on the plank, but he was starting to look like a ballet dancer at barre, one leg extended backward. He was becoming not agile, I thought, but flexible.)

Near the end of the class, while running another drill, Willow refused to mount the pause box as well, which normally he would be bouncing up onto with ease. Perhaps it had become tainted by its association with the inclined plank? Whatever the case, something had shifted in my dog's head from positive to negative. There was something determinedly resigned in his manner. He had developed a doggie mental block. He had decided to refuse and to dig in his paws. Now it wasn't just his ears and his tail that were down, his head and neck were involved, too. He was carrying them so low that his chin nearly scraped the earth. The glow and loft were gone from his golden coat. He was avoiding all eye contact. He looked like a stray collie, a beaten dog, a dog nobody loved.

The leaders of the pack—Sue and me—we were disappointed in him, and he knew it.

How could he tell how unhappy with him we were? I remember wondering this at the time. Sue and I had never scolded or reprimanded him. We had given him only treats and praise, and for the tiniest of progress. We had asked him to mount these two obstacles only in the nicest way. And even when Sue was calling him a "poop," I could hear her carefully modulating her voice so that her tone remained light and cheerful and affectionate (and I, at this point, imitated everything she did, down to aping her Boston accent). In short, we had never given Willow anything but encouragement and yummy treats. How could he possibly appreciate our disappointment? And yet he did. He knew.

If this were simply a dog not doing what I wanted—*defying my will*, as I once would have thought of it—I don't think this first setback would have affected me in quite the way it did. But as I have said, I had begun to see Willow in a very different way—as this intelligent, thinking creature participating in his own training. He *wanted* to do it, I knew; he enjoyed the work and maintaining that keen, subtle herding dog focus. And when his rapt attention went away, when he put his head down and refused to look me in the eye, it was a depressing feeling. It was as if a warm golden light beamed upon me had suddenly switched off.

I knew that Willow wasn't defying my will. He loved the agility training. But the motivation, the food, the fun, they weren't enough to get him over whatever hurdle had gone up between his ears. If he was a human being, I thought, you could just have asked him—and found out what it was that was bothering him. But he wasn't. He was a big inexperienced adolescent dog with a mysterious grey sponge of brain inside his flat head, so very different from my own, so much more nose and presence, so much less abstract and verbal. I gazed at him in his unhappiness and wondered what it was about his doggie experience of that plank that was troubling him.

With Sue's help, I tried to puzzle it out. What was it with these two big dogs and the inclined plank? I could think of a couple of possibilities:

Both of these dogs, both Willow and the Rottweiler, had trouble with the plank before, at the beginning, and I now began to wonder if they had never really gotten comfortable with it. Though they had both seemed to be walking the level plank happily before Sue tipped it up, I wondered now if I had merely been a poor observer. Perhaps if I had studied them more closely, I would have seen a hunched shoulder, a drooping tail, a quivering ear, all signs of doggie anxiety.

Maybe it was the same old trouble with their back ends that Sue had pointed out in the first class. The larger dogs seemed to take more for granted the position of their hindquarters than did the smaller, more compact dogs. Perhaps this was because they had a greater weight to cart around. They seemed to depend more heavily upon their back feet to power them forward, or to climb, and to require a wider stance for better traction. They also seemed to prefer not to notice the position of their back paws, something that was of course necessary on the narrow board. The problem, I decided, wasn't climbing per se, but rather was the narrowness of the plank.

The big boys *did like* to climb—that wasn't the trouble. That's why Willow enjoyed the A-frame so much. He could power up over the top, pushing with his back feet and pulling with his front feet—in fact, he looked rather monkeyish doing this, pulling himself up over the top with his front arms that way. He also seemed to enjoy jumping, which like climbing the A-frame required less delicacy of action. But asking him to hop his back feet up onto a narrow balance beam required him to perform what was I think for him a thoroughly unnatural function—to attend to the position of his back feet.

I noticed something else, too. The plank vibrated. But it vibrated *a whole lot more* under the weight of the bigger dogs, and bounced noticeably when tilted up against the pause box. These were both big dogs—have I mentioned how big? At a year old, Willow already stood twenty-six inches at the shoulder, the maximum size under the AKC breed standard for a rough collie, and he still had a good six months of growing left to do. Eventually he would top out at about twenty-seven or twenty-eight inches at the shoulder, and eighty-five to ninety pounds. I remember going to a dog show later with a friend and remarking to her how small all the collies looked to me. "That's because Willow's so *big*," she pointed out. And the Rottweiler, he dwarfed even Willow. He was a large, powerfully built animal, similar to a mastiff, but colored black with liver toned eyebrows and cheek spots. He stood at least another two inches taller than Willow at the shoulder and was much more massive through the chest and body. His legs and paws were twice as wide as Willow's slender collie gams. The bigger dogs, they really shake that plank, I thought.

That was it, I decided. That was what was holding the big boys back. It was the back end problem combined with the extra bounce and vibration from their greater weight shaking the plank. But what to do about it?

Sue felt bad—I could see that she did. She was a demanding teacher, but a benevolent one, and she had taken full note of how unhappy Willow looked. She didn't like to see this in one of her canine students, this face of defeat. She stayed after class and worked with him. A lower pause box. A lower plank. At last Willow got up on the pause box (happily, relieved), but not the plank, still not the plank. Sue and I discussed it. We must build up his confidence, she said, her voice grave. So grave you'd think she was discussing cardiac surgery. Train at home, she told me. Put the plank right back down on the ground this week and let him walk on it. The failure, she said, was not in the dog; the failure was in the training. We went too fast, she said. We have to go back and build up his confidence slowly. Trust and confidence are everything in agility training. And so I had my marching orders. When I got home, I was to go to the local lumberyard and buy a plank just like this one, twelve feet long and ten inches wide. I was to paint a nonskid surface on it so that Willow wouldn't slip. And then we were to start over. Slowly.

I left class determined to try these things. Yes, I thought, we will try. Still, I couldn't help but wonder if this was going to be the thing that would end Willow's agility career before it had ever really begun. Was this the thing that would stop him? And was there any point in proceeding if he was already having this much trouble?

I felt very much the way I did when my son turned out not to like soccer or baseball, the town sports all the other kids seemed to love. "I'm the worst one," my son would say, which wasn't entirely true. He wasn't the *worst* one. A few other kids were worse. "That's all right," my husband and I said. "You don't have to do it. That's okay." And we bit back our disappointment. Not every kid likes sports, we told ourselves. Ours loves to read and play chess. He's really smart. And he's a nice person, a sweet kid. Still, oh, how we wanted him to step up to the plate and knock it out of the ballpark. We did. You know that we did.

There's a concept in agility training called "going back to kindergarten." The idea, which probably is not unique to dog training, is that if your dog gets scared or confused, or simply refuses to perform the tasks you are asking of him, then you need to back up and make things easier again. It's a matter of building up skills and confidence. You can't walk a tightrope halfway. You can't jump out of a plane tentatively or sort of. If you are going to do a high-risk activity, then you have to train. You have to build up your skills until you are sure you have them down. And then you need to commit to the activity. You need to go out and perform with assurance and authority. You need to believe. There's no doing it halfway.

The same is true for a big dog walking a high balance beam. He must have confidence to do it. He can't bail out partway. This is almost always a matter of preparation and training. Of building the necessary skills and gaining confidence. Going back to kindergarten is about going back to an easier step where the dog can feel he has that confidence and assurance. Where he can be successful. Then, slowly, you raise the bar.

Success builds on itself. If a dog is successful at one level, then he is much more likely to succeed at the next level when things get tougher. If he loses it, gets scared, balks, freaks out, then you went too fast. Go back to kindergarten.

Success builds on itself, but so does failure—as I had seen with Willow and the plank. At first he couldn't do the plank, and then soon he couldn't do the pause box either. If you fail at one thing, suddenly before you looms the possibility of failing at everything else. That's why it's so important to keep winning, even if it means you must go really, really slowly.

This, then, was the theory. This was what Sue was telling me.

If I had been through this training before, perhaps I would have understood that sooner or later this happens to nearly every agility dog. At some point in training, nearly every dog hits a wall, no matter what his breed or level of talent. He falls or gets scared for some reason, and has to go back to an earlier step and build up his confidence again before going on. Often this happens when a dog is first introduced to the seesaw or "teeter," which from the dog's perspective looks exactly like the "up" plank of the dogwalk—until he hits the tipping point and the board falls out from under him and strikes the ground with a loud *bang*. It is at this point that a lot of dogs have to go back and learn planks and dogwalks all over again. Usually with slow, careful training almost any dog can be coaxed through these stages successfully, but with some sensitive dogs it can take a lot of patience on the handler's part.

Of course, never having done this training before, I didn't know any of this. Sue was probably telling me, but it wasn't sinking in, the way things don't if you haven't encountered them before. I knew only that Willow and I were holding up the bottom of the class again. Like my dog, I could see all those other dogs popping easily up that narrow slope, all but the Rottie and my stupid, untalented collie (or so I thought at the time). And it wasn't lost on me at this point that this failure was very probably as much my fault as it was his—that I had probably failed in some way as his handler.

After our setback with the inclined plank, I remember a very long trip home, driving up a very dark Route 3 in an unaccountably foul mood. This was, after all, only dog training. How upset should I really get? But I was upset. *Very.*

I was under strict instructions from Sue not to take my disappointment out on my dog (which many people apparently do in these situations, and I certainly was tempted). And so I drove home, flopped on my bed, and pounded a pillow. I was a real baby about it, a real brat. I kicked, I complained. A tear or two may even have leaked from my eye. I was finding this setback for some reason inordinately humiliating and frustrating. On our last walk of the evening, I probably jerked Willow's neck a bit too hard with his leash, wanting perhaps to slide back into my old ways of choke collars and domination that had made me feel so good about myself.

Years later, I am still trying to puzzle out why I took this so hard. I think now that—like my sudden ambitions for agility—it had to do with my having done dog training when I was a kid. I think that I had managed to grow up and get into my middle years with the vanity—one of those little vanities we all have—that I was good at dog training, and that I was good generally with animals. It was a vanity that had never really been put to the test, since I had never done any competitive dog training since that time, either in obedience or agility—just made my own dogs "mind"—not a terribly difficult thing to do since I have always had tractable herding breed dogs. So when it turned out that I wasn't especially good at dog training, or at least, I should say, that both Willow and I had a lot to learn—a whole lot more than many of the other dogs and handlers in Sue Reed's agility class—it took a big chunk out of my self-image for a time. In my own mind, one moment it was all Willow's fault, and I wanted to get out my old choke collar and strangle my uncooperative collie. The next moment it was all my own fault, and I was a bad handler, was bad at dog training, and bad with animals, and all that wonderful parental approval I'd felt after winning that little red ribbon when I was a kid— my mother had made a huge fuss over me at the time—went away, leaving me feeling worthless and ashamed. It all sounds a little silly, sitting here writing about it today, but I have to tell you, at the time I felt truly miserable.

I wonder now if I would have gotten through it if Sue Reed had been less imperious and directive in her orders of what I was to do—or if I simply would have gotten mad, thrown up my hands, and dropped out of class. But the whole time I had her stern, resolute voice ringing in my ears, telling me exactly what I had to do to get around this problem. And so I did it. To this day, I still don't know quite why. Say Sue was the coach, the boss. Say that I could see she knew a whole lot more about dog training than I did.

And so I went to the local lumberyard and bought a heavy pine plank. I painted a rough surface on it using green paint mixed with sand. And then I put it right back down on the ground, and let Willow walk on it for several days, before putting it up a mere four inches, on bricks. And yet even as I did this, even as I started right back down on the ground with him and worked slowly up from there, I recall feeling extremely depressed. I didn't think it would work. In fact, I was *sure* it wouldn't. Either Willow can do this, I thought to myself, or he can't. He can't, and so why are we bothering with all of this nonsense?

And yet, for some reason—call it my blind faith in Sue Reed's magical dog training powers—I *did* do it. Yes, I did. I started working Willow up slowly, slowly. So slowly you wouldn't believe. So slowly that it hurts my poor brain to think about it even now. First the plank was on bricks, then on a few books, then on cinder blocks laid sideways, and so forth.

And the whole time I was thinking, *This is not going to work.*

Nine

How did I get into this in the first place? That's always the question you ask yourself, isn't it, when things go wrong? *Why was it I decided to try a sport called agility with a dog so untalented he can't even climb up on the lowest, most basic plank?*

All week long, as I began working with Willow, I chewed on myself this way. It's not like I don't have a busy life, I thought. I write, I teach, I go to school—at the time of this agility training I was pursuing my master's in creative writing at a local college. I have a young son, and a husband, and a house to take care of. I'm a grownup with responsibilities. So why was I spending every Tuesday evening hanging around with the family dog? It's not like I didn't have a few other things to do with my time.

Human motivation is an odd thing. Why we do what we do. In my case, I was bitten by the dog-training bug as a child.

My family has always had dogs, a succession of canines that has included golden retrievers, a German shepherd, and a series of beagles that my father and grandfather took rabbit hunting—slow, steady dogs with talented noses. These were the family dogs. They were not *mine*. The first dog that I ever fell in love with, and that truly felt like *my dog*, was that timid black and white border collie, Tippy.

We were visiting my grandfather's dairy farm in the Adirondack foothills one weekend when this dog adopted us. (My grandfather—you remember him—he of the drowned puppies and kittens). I must have been about eight at the time. Tippy was a small, cringing female with large intelligent brown eyes, her body entirely covered in a thin sheath of glossy blue-black fur, except for a small white blaze on her chest and the white tip at the end of her tail, for which she was named. Actually, if you look, most collies have this white tip at the ends of their tails, dubbed by collie fanciers as "the Shepherd's Lantern," presumably because it is there for the sheep to follow home in the falling dusk.

I don't know for sure where my grandfather got this dog—I gather she was intended to replace his old cow dog, Shep, a muddy-looking shepherding dog of indeterminate breed and stable disposition that had recently passed on. The story we heard—which may or may not have been apocryphal—was that Tippy's old owner hadn't wanted her, and that she had been tied outside his trailer for weeks and repeatedly kicked. Perhaps this story was true, perhaps not. She certainly was timid, but shyness may have been in her nature, for I have since learned that excessive shyness is a common temperament fault in border collies. In any event, Tippy cowered in a perpetual crouch, and if my father or any man strode near her, a trickle of urine would creep across the linoleum floor as surely as the mercury rises in hot weather. My grandfather was disgusted with this beaten waif and seemed determined to be rid of her. If we hadn't taken her, in all likelihood she would have been escorted out back and shot—a fact that I'm sure was not lost on my softhearted mother.

Tippy was so shy and incontinent—a condition that I should note later cleared up with a round of antibiotics and a little love—that at first my parents didn't want to take her, at least my father didn't want to, for it meant facing his own father's disapproval. But my twin brother and I played with her all that warm June afternoon—some game in the long mountain grass involving a thin black and white dog and a rope. I think we were pretending Tippy was a wild horse that we were breaking and riding. I have a picture of this somewhere in my attic, taken by my mother, the colors long since bleached out, Tippy's shiny black fur oxidized to a navy blue. In it two children are bent over a dog, the boy dressed in cowboy hat, vest, and holster and looking tough, the girl a skinny little figure in rumpled cotton shorts, her dark eyes worried beneath frowning brows, her mouth serious. (If I had to guess, I'd bet she was worried that the cowboy was being a bit rough with the horse.) Tippy, as I recall, was a good sport, taking the rope in her teeth and chewing it like a bit, and when we pulled, tugging back like anything. She made a great wild horse, a bronco that pulled and bucked but never really ran away.

When the visit was over and it was time to go home, Tim and I chorused *please, please,* couldn't we keep her, *pleeeeease.* In later years, when my mother would tell this story, she would get to this point, and pause, and tell you with a droll smile that she was intending to say, *No, absolutely not, no way. We don't need another dog.* We already had the two beagles at the time. Then, she would say—with a bit more drama creeping into her voice (she did theater in college)—Tippy made a noise. A sort of long descending whine or whimper that sounded for all the world exactly like "please?" *Pleeease.* Just the way my brother and I had said it. *Pleeease.*

This is, I am sure, one of those stories that improves with age. Still, we did get to keep the dog. I like to think that my mother wanted to keep Tippy herself, and that she took the dog's whine as "please" so that she could do just that in the face of my grandfather's disapproval. Ah, the power of narrative! For how could you say "no" after something like that? When the dog had nearly burst into speech that way? At any rate, it was this dark trembling creature that I took to my first community obedience training classes at age nine.

It was, as I have noted, strictly jerk and release choke collar training back then, straight out of World War II. My memories are dim, dreamy. There could have been five classes, or twenty. The course could have lasted a few weeks or a year—I don't recall. I climb up into this memory as into an observation turret and peer out through the fisheye lens of remembrance onto a huge windy field behind our local high school. In the foreground there is sparse, crackly grass too thin to hold down the dry Upstate New York dirt of my childhood summers, which swirls up in clouds of dust with each gust of the ever-present wind. My long, curly hair wheels about my head in different directions, and I hold Tippy's braided rope leash in my hands. Arrayed about the field, impossibly distant, yet somehow close-by, are many adults and their dogs. The dogs are of every shape and size, bassets, springers, bloodhounds, goldens, Labs, mutts. I am the only kid; Tippy the only collie dog. We are both terrified, and lean hard against each other. My mother stands at the sidelines behind a rope, impossibly small and far away, her bouffant flattened by wind.

I'm sure there was a choke collar around Tippy's neck, but I don't remember it. I recall only her furry body pressed against my left knee and thigh, a ghostly black dog in my memory. I recall the heat of her on my leg, a small dark furnace burning furiously in her fear. It's hard to imagine us heeling, leaned together this way, but we must have. I remember how Tippy's ability to absorb the training seemed almost magical. I didn't know then what a border collie was or how they are driven to work. I didn't know that they almost train themselves.

As a child, I remember being convinced that I could talk to animals. Many children have these Dr. Dolittle fantasies. I believed them. There were horses fenced in a pasture behind our house, fat ponies being boarded, and a few trotters from a nearby racing stable. I remember that on hot summer afternoons I would perch on the middle rail of the back fence, a few lumps of sugar in my pocket, and neigh at them. Now and then a horse would answer back. I was sure we were talking horse talk. It was like that with Tippy, only more so. I knew we spoke a secret dog language that let us understand each other. My certainty of this was like a gleaming gem I carried deep in my chest, a nugget of power that made animals knowable to me and that allowed them to speak my name and, sometimes, permitted me to answer back. The world was an enchanted place when I was eight or nine, and training Tippy was the proof of my abilities.

At the last obedience class of the session, there was a competition. Ribbons would be bestowed upon the winners. Gradually the other dogs and their handlers were whittled away until only three pairs of us remained, three humans with their three dogs. I recall that one was a tall man with a large German shepherd dog whose gaze was permanently riveted upon his face. Then, of course, there was Tippy and me. I don't recall the third dog. There may as well have been no third dog. In my mind, it was all Tippy and me competing against the tall man with the German shepherd. I remember that there was a hot duel at heeling and recalls. I remember that the German shepherd won, but that it was close, and that afterward Tippy and I got a bright red ribbon, which I have long since lost. My mother said that everyone was rooting for us because I was the only kid, but probably it was only her rooting for us. She was ecstatic that we'd beaten all those grownups and had nearly run away with the blue. And she was amused that some of the adults were mad at being beaten by a kid that way. I remember her saying that if I could do this well as a child, just imagine when I was older. And me? I felt a kind of fierce pride for Tippy and myself. In my mind, that little red ribbon was proof of the magic we shared.

There is a sad end to this story, a terrible end—though in truth I don't remember much of it. A few months after the obedience classes ended, Tippy was run down by a speeding car in front of our house and killed before my eyes. We lived out in the country, and nobody tied dogs up. Things like that happened. The accident must have been too painful, for I seem to have blocked out the memory of it. I carry in my head only a few snatches from afterward: How the vet came in his white van to take away my beloved dead dog. I remember, like the afterglow of a flashbulb at the back of the eye, the white doors at the rear of the van as they glanced open, and the vet hoisting Tippy's lifeless body upside down by her paws into the cool, sterile interior, and, as he did, the terrible fascination of the dark blood that poured from her mouth in unimaginable quantity, as if pumped from an underground spring.

It is perhaps the ugliness of this retained image that has for all time assured Tippy's foremost place in my memory among the pantheon of Great Dogs I Have Known, and my own permanent interest in dog training and in trying to communicate with animals.

I'm grown up now, and I don't believe in magic anymore, do I? I couldn't possibly.

But here's the thing: We aren't just who we are now. We are always also everyone who we have ever been. Somewhere down deep, I'm still the kid who believes that she can talk to animals, and who has the proof of it in the shape of a small, cowering black and white border collie.

As an adult, I gaze with disdain upon the people on TV who really believe such things. You've seen them. The Pet Psychic, and the others who claim to believe in such Mr. Ed style communication with animals. These would-be Dr. Dolittles make me wince as I flip past them, switching channels. They strike me, at best, as cases of arrested development, and at worst as charlatans, and in any event as misguided or fraudulent and not to be credited. These days they also seem to me an insult to the Sue Reeds and Karen Pryors of the world, the real animal trainers who have developed such a deep and authentic understanding of the animals they work with that what they do almost seems magical. The truth is that communication with animals can be had, but it isn't sorcery. It is a matter of hard work, technical understanding, experience, and perhaps more than a little native skill. Still, when I see these people on TV—I have to admit that I understand the impulse. Truly, I do.

It is interesting to me now, thinking back upon this story from my childhood. Plainly when I was a kid, I was living out some kind of fantasy about communicating with animals, and perhaps that's all it was—a fantasy—and one I apparently left behind as I grew up. What I took into adulthood with me were the forced training methods I had learned, and the idea that dog training was about dominating an animal and bending it to your will. That it was about choke collars and jerked leashes. How did this happen? I'm not sure. Somewhere along the way, the relationship I had with Tippy began to seem childish, and the forced methods of training I had been taught began to make more sense. Something about developing the authority of an adult, perhaps—and this made me doubt what I had experienced, and convinced me that a heavier hand was the right way. I guess I didn't realize what I'd lost until I got it back. And getting it back—well, that was a process.

I wonder now, though, having done this agility training, if in my childhood innocence I didn't have an openness to animals back then that I had lost as an adult. As a grownup, I clearly had lost track of the notion that dog training might be about communicating with an animal, and not just forcing it to do my bidding. Oddly, on some level, I think that this story can be seen as a trip I have taken to return myself to some original state of grace and understanding with animals. Or perhaps it is simply a journey back to a more egalitarian view of them, as creatures of equal worth, if very different from ourselves, yet with whom interchange is possible.

I wonder if, as a child, I really was only caught up in my own infantile fantasies, or if I was more naturally astute and aware about animals, and willing to give them my full attention, and pay heed to what they were doing and how they felt, in a way that adults usually aren't. I think now that perhaps we adults erect unnecessary barriers between ourselves and the animals in our care. We see them only as simple beasts to be commanded and controlled in a way that children do not. Perhaps this accounts for the weird genius children often seem to exhibit around our four-legged friends.

Ten

A week had passed, and it was time for our next agility class. All week, Willow and I had been training at home. We had trained in short sessions, but regularly, sometimes twice or three times a day. I had put the plank right back down on the ground as I had been instructed to do and let Willow walk on it for a couple of days, not a brick or a stone under it. For several days, big treats and praise for only this. Then I raised the plank on bricks, just a couple of inches. More treats and praise. Slowly, slowly it began to work, though I'm not sure I even quite noticed this fact at first—I was still so filled with disdain for both myself and my dog. I was a hopelessly untalented dog trainer, in my own estimation, and Willow—Willow was an effete, useless purebred. My old ambitions, though, must still have been driving me, for grimly, methodically, I did everything that Sue had told me to do. At the least sign of doggie anxiety, a flipped ear or an urge to sniff or walk away, we stopped right there and worked at that height until Willow looked totally comfortable and was bouncing up happily on the plank. Then we continued on.

Willow himself seemed not especially to notice or care about my own bad mood. While I was working away grimly on him, my ambition warring with my injured pride, he was busily succeeding at walking low planks and gulping yummy dog treats. Chunks of bacon and ham, a few pieces of cold salmon. Actually, he was looking downright happy about things. These tasks were easy, and the rewards were great. Who wouldn't be delighted?

Once I had the plank up about eight inches off the ground, set on cinder blocks laid sideways, I decided to begin tilting it a bit, since inclined planks seemed to be the real problem at that point. I rested one end of the plank on the first step of the two steps that connected our low back deck to the lawn. The first step was only about four inches high. Willow, though, had apparently decided that he didn't like inclined planks of any sort, and looked askance at even this low tilt. But, in the end, it was so low that even he couldn't refuse—not for calves liver and the leftover filet mignon from a friend's wedding. A little more steak and soon the plank was up on the next step—a mere eight inches off the ground, and Willow was walking on it without trouble. This was where things stood when it was time for our next agility class.

That week, Sue brought out the big dogwalk for the first time—the high, thirty-foot-long bridge. All of the other dogs were ready for it, with the possible exception of the Rottweiler—though even he was standing in line to try the dogwalk, I saw. Not Willow, though. Sue said that she wanted to see him walking *both* the low level plank *and* the inclined plank comfortably before we even thought about the big dogwalk. And so she sent us—Willow and me—off to train at the side of the arena on the other two planks, while she coached the rest of the class through their first cracks at the big dogwalk, which at this point was set at the fairly low height of about two and one-half to three feet off the ground.

I started by taking Willow back to the level plank, and was heartened to see him pounce right up on it. Our work over the course of the week had clearly paid off. He looked so good on the level plank that when he had walked along it two or three times, I decided to gird myself for failure and take him over to the inclined plank again, the one leaned up against the pause box, standing exactly where it had been the week before when our troubles first began. I knew now, from working with Willow at home, that he had taken a real aversion to inclined planks, and this one was much higher than the eight-inch rise off our back deck that we had been practicing on. This plank was still twenty inches high at one end, and since we had already failed at it once, it looked even more daunting this week than it had the week before. On the other hand, Willow had been trotting happily up and down the lower inclined plank back home, and so I decided to give it a try. What the hell, right? At this point, it felt as if we didn't have much to lose. We clearly were on the verge of washing out of this agility class—at least in my own opinion.

I led Willow to the inclined plank and asked him almost lackadaisically to mount it. To my amazement, he went up quick as anything. He still crouched a little, and his ears were twitching a bit, but he did it, and received his treat up on the pause box. Then he turned around and came trotting back down. Suddenly, he whipped around and trotted right back up the plank a second time, and stood looking at me from the pause box, waiting for his treat. I remember feeling almost stunned with surprise. I was astonished that the work we had done over the week had produced this effect. I probably shouldn't have been so surprised, but I was. This felt almost like something Willow had done by himself, with very little involvement from me. At least with very little emotional involvement—which maybe was where we had to get to in order for us to succeed at planks. For me to stop pushing Willow—though of course I didn't see this at the time. Over the course of the past week, I had spent most of my emotional life somewhere off in my own head, nursing my injured pride. And by the time we got to class, I think I had almost begun not to care if Willow did this or not. But while I was off caught up in my own little emotional drama, apparently my dog had been busy mastering planks.

As Willow was climbing up the inclined plank for a third time, and was looking more and more solid at it, here came the big Rottweiler and his handsome blond handler, over to join us. The Rottie was still slipping his back paws off the upslope of the dogwalk, and so—like Willow—he had been sent off to the side by Sue for more plank work. I could see that the Rottie's handler, like me, had made sure to bring a big bag of especially tasty treats to class—to help get her dog over his aversion to planks. I don't remember exactly what she had, but we'll say that it was a big bag of beef liver chunks. Something that would really appeal to a dog. Whatever it was, Willow smelled it, and as the Rottie neared us, the two big dogs eyed each other and sniffed each others' jowls, each apparently checking to see what rewards the other dog was getting. The Rottie's handler and I discussed it, and we decided that we would have our dogs trade off turns. And so we began training together.

Willow, by now, was looking quite solid at the inclined plank—His tail, which previously had been tucked low, was rising and waving again, and so he went first. Having the big Rottweiler join us seemed to have some sort of effect on him. He seemed suddenly more avid and eager. Perhaps he was afraid that the other big dog would get his treats if he didn't get up on the pause box fast enough. And so he sped up the plank and wolfed down the chicken chunks I offered him, all the while eyeing his rival. Now it was the Rottie's turn. He walked up the plank with a deliberate swagger and quickly gobbled down the chunks of beef liver his handler held out to him, his eyes pinned firmly upon Willow. The dogs traded another couple of turns, and then suddenly something happened. It got really competitive.

The Rottie pounded up the plank, straight up to the pause box. Big jackpot of meat for that kind of speed. Not to be out-done, Willow raced up to the box, twirled, and then raced back down, his paws solid and strong, pounding the board. From there, it was as if the two dogs were obsessed. They strained toward the inclined plank while waiting their turns, and then pounced on it when we let them go, riding it, striding it, tak-ing command. They couldn't get enough of it and wanted to do it again and again. With their big paws whacking down, the plank became like a living thing. It wiggled, bounced, and writhed with the weight of those two great dogs thundering up and down. The Rottie's handler and I gazed at each other, our eyes wide with amazement. *Are you seeing this?*—we silently mouthed to each other.

The two dogs now actually seemed to *like* the vibration and bounce of the plank; that was the strange thing. They seemed to relish it, to be passionate about it, to want to take control of it. Their big paws banged and slammed as they raced up and down, making it shiver and jump and hop. Somewhere along the line they seemed to have stopped caring about the treats. There was some sort of macho competition in progress here—two young male dogs issuing challenges to each other.

At one point, I heard a low thunderous growl emanate from somewhere deep in the Rottweiler's chest as the two dogs continued pounding up and down the board. All I could do was stand back and laugh, and think what a kick this was to watch.

The temptation was to take both dogs straight over to the big dogwalk while they were still on a roll, but when I led Willow over to the end of the other drill line, Sue shook her head and waved me away. Before class ended, she would tell me to keep working on planks at home for another week, and upon reflection, I had to agree. Willow needed to keep winning. We needed to make sure he was absolutely solid before trying the dogwalk—which at this point looked really high and long to me. I was in no particular rush at that moment to court more failure. I wanted to enjoy where we were and the progress we had made, and to take a break. It was such a relief to have things going right again.

I should say something here about the tone with which Sue was now addressing me. She seemed pleased with the progress that Willow and I had made over the past week, but she also seemed a bit chilly—or no, not chilly—that's a little strong. Rather, she was looking at me a bit critically, as if waiting to see how I would react to all of this. She seemed to be withholding judgment on whether Willow and I would be able to succeed at this dog agility or not, and her judgment seemed to be directed mainly at me, and not at my dog. She seemed to be gauging whether I would have the good sense to tell where my dog was at this moment, and not to push him too fast out of my own desires and ambitions. In retrospect, I understand this. At this point—to her—Willow probably looked promising enough. But there were real questions about me—about whether I would be able to get over my own ego and my need to push my dog to do things before he was really ready. I suspect that, to her mind, I still was not observing my dog keenly enough to see how he was doing. I was still trying to push him, and was making my training decisions based upon how *I was feeling* and my own need to succeed, rather than on *what was right for my dog*. My request to take him to the big dogwalk right away was probably just confirmation of this for her. Of course, I didn't appreciate any of this at the time—or at least not much of it—and I left class probably in too good a mood, delighted with the way we were coming back after our little setback.

After class ended, Willow still had energy to burn. He was back to his old self and then some. He started to zoom madly about the parking lot, racing around with that funny porpoisey running gait collies have that has to do with them being crossbred with coursing dogs like borzois and greyhounds in order to gain their tall physical stature early in the creation of the breed. I know that you aren't supposed to project human emotions onto dogs, but if this wasn't dog happiness, then I don't know what is. Willow had just done everything I had asked of him in class, and he had also survived his plank duel with that huge macho Rottweiler. To calm him down, I called him over and gave him a full all-over body scratch—something every collie I have ever known has always loved, with their heavy itchy coats—and something that for the past week I had probably been too self-involved to do for him. He nibbled my arms and hands with his front teeth, the way collies do—"flea-ing me," as it is called—and he talked a bit, complaining about what he'd been through and telling me how much happier he was now. Okay, he didn't *really* talk, but collies make these funny crooning noises when vocalizing their pleasure that we call "Wookie Noises" at home, because they sound exactly like the noises made by Chewbacca in the *Star Wars* movies. The noises Willow made that night sounded a note of both relief and complaint, a crooning, growling song that was rather like a bear playing a cello.

On our way home, still soaring with our success, I blasted loud rock music on the radio and tapped out the time with my thumbs using the steering wheel as my drum kit. On the radio, I remember Melissa Etheridge belting out something about walking *across a fire for you-ooh*, and I sang along loudly. I rode home loving life, loving my dog, and all the way, racing up a dark Route 3, the white lines of the expressway unwound in front of me like long ghostly prize ribbons, the colors having run out over the years.

Eleven

If I was really serious about taking Willow to the big dog-walk at our next agility class—the last class of our fall session with Sue Reed—then I should have been training all week with him, doing planks every day with lots of short practices and big praise and treats. Instead, I didn't. Maybe I was afraid that I would do something to ruin Willow's newfound confidence. Perhaps I was just resting on our laurels and being lazy. Whatever the case, I didn't train him during the week, at least not much. I ran him over the level plank in the yard maybe twice. It was still sitting out there in front of the house, resting on its cinder blocks, and we passed it coming and going in the morning on our way to and from our walks. And so I ran him down the length of it a couple of times, and that was it. The next thing I knew, Tuesday had arrived, and it was time to go back to agility class again.

When we got to class, there were other drills to run, and we didn't get back to the dogwalk until we were nearing the end of this final class. Again, as with the previous week, Sue sent Willow and me back to the inclined plank for more work. Willow, though, had by now utterly conquered the inclined plank, repeating his performance of the week before, and so Sue had no choice but to let us in line for the big dogwalk, something that I was of course pushing for, having determined that our prior success was no fluke. I was incapable at this point of not pushing Willow—not with every other dog in the class now doing the long bridge with greater or lesser degrees of success, including the Rottweiler, who had twice succeeded in crossing the dogwalk, albeit slowly and with lots of encouragement.

As we joined the drill line, was it my imagination, or was everyone watching to see how we would do? Perhaps it was only my own self-consciousness and my vanity that made me think that all the other handlers had observed every turn of our plank troubles, and that they were taking great pleasure in our failures. I found myself in line behind the woman with the pretty-faced sheltie. She turned to me while we waited and with a confidential air told me a story: She had this friend, it seemed, who had a big collie *just like Willow*. This person had gotten to *just this point* with her dog, she said, when this collie fell off the dogwalk. "Took a big fall," she said. She glanced over at the dogwalk that we were about to try, which this week Sue had cranked up to three and one-half or four feet off the ground (the other dogs were ready for it), then looked back at Willow. "That was it for him and agility," she concluded. "So be careful." As she said this, she placed a lot of emphasis on the word *care*. At the time, I recall thinking that this other handler was being incredibly obnoxious and condescending, telling me this story right before Willow and I were about to try the big dogwalk for the first time—a piece of equipment with which her own dog was having absolutely no trouble whatsoever. Talk about shaking someone's confidence at the wrong moment. Now, though, I think that she was probably right. I was taking a big risk putting Willow up on the dogwalk at that point.

Collies are extremely sensitive by nature, and one bad fall easily could have been it for Willow. And given all the trouble he'd already had with planks, the dogwalk should have been set much lower the first time he tried it—at two feet, not four—so that he could hop off if he needed to. At any rate, I glared at this woman and steeled myself for what I was sure was coming. Her little sheltie popped right up the dogwalk, of course, with the sure-footed grace of a trapeze artist, and trotted the full length moving fast and sure, prancing actually. When they were done, they came back and stood by us, and the woman was laughing. "Oh, she loves to climb," she said apologetically, explaining her dog's success to the less successful. "She's like a cat, always up on the table or the back of the couch." Needless to say, this was not what I needed to hear. Willow had never even come close to getting up on the back of the couch. Or the table. And at his size, he never would.

Now it was our turn. Sue was standing alongside us as we approached the dogwalk for the first time. She was watching Willow as he moved toward it, squinting at him as intensely as if she were gauging, say, the green bubble on a spirit level. She must have approved of what she saw, for she let us continue. I don't think she would have thought twice about stopping us if she hadn't liked the way Willow looked. And so I directed Willow to go to it. "Dogwalk!" I commanded him in a light cheerful tone (which thinly veiled my own trepidation), and swung my arm in the direction of this thirty-foot bridge of wood that he was to mount and traverse. I walked along with him as he approached the up-plank, my pocket full of meat, bracing myself as he began to climb. Actually, no, that's not right—I didn't brace myself. The truth is, I felt rather detached from my emotions at that moment. It no longer seemed to matter so much whether Willow succeeded or failed. If he fell and his agility career was over, so be it. We had been through so much, it seemed, and I had put so much pressure on myself to succeed—on both of us to succeed—that I think failure at that point would have been something of a relief. I wasn't afraid of Willow hurting himself. He was a big dog, and a jump or fall off the dogwalk wasn't really so much higher than him jumping out of my Outback, though it clearly could have scared him. And so I strode alongside him and watched, almost curiously, to see how he would do.

Willow seemed not at all nervous. Slowly and surely he climbed the up-plank, and plucked a treat from my palm with his teeth. Then he edged out upon the high crossbeam, too high and too narrow for a big dog like him, or so I thought. He was crouching a little, but he stepped forward with the sure-footed (if slightly tippy) stance of a gymnast. As he crossed the high plank he picked up speed, so that by the time he reached the downslope, he was almost trotting.

I don't think I quite appreciated how badly I had wanted him to do it until after he was already down on solid earth again. I felt suddenly shaky, high, and a little weightless—as if I had just walked a high wire myself. Sue was smiling, pleased, but Willow's success wasn't as big a deal for her as it was for me. *All in a day's work* was the expression on her face. One obstacle mastered; now on to the next thing. She had probably seen this kind of progress a hundred times before—a young dog being taught new skills and gaining confidence. Willow repeated his performance several more times without a hitch, becoming faster and surer with each traverse of the dogwalk.

And so we had done it, I seemed almost belatedly to realize. Willow and me. The practice had paid off. Willow's new confidence had carried him up and over the dogwalk. And with Sue's help, I had—almost in spite of myself—gotten inside my dog's head and figured out what was bothering him—his back end and the vibration of the plank. We had spent the necessary time at home that week when we trained so hard building up Willow's plank skills, and then he had overcome his fear of the bounce and vibration of the inclined plank that wonderful night in his macho contest with the Rottweiler. From the outside, it probably seems pretty simple and perhaps even anticlimactic, but from the inside the experience felt like a revelation to me. This is how it's done, I finally began to understand, in what seemed a flash of insight. You have to watch your dog closely. You have to figure out what's going on inside that mysterious cave that is his head. And then you work with that. You pay attention to his tail, his body, his head, his face, his ears. You take note of where and when it is that he seems to get nervous and balky. You can tell a lot, just by watching a dog. Maybe not all, but a lot. Dogs are such physical creatures, that if you watch them carefully, a great deal shows.

I was so happy that evening, with my dog and myself, that I didn't even care when Sue told me that Willow and I would have to repeat the beginners class with her partner, Cheryl Wells. The other dogs, it seemed, were all moving up to the advanced beginners class. Sue, though, wanted to be absolutely sure that Willow was solid on the dogwalk before we proceeded on.

In retrospect, I can see how close we nearly were to failing. I think now that I had tried to push Willow too far, too fast. He was very young, and he needed to go slower. I think if I had tried to push him any faster, he might have stumbled and fallen that day on the dogwalk, and we never would have gotten any further in agility. After this—in all of our months of training—Willow would never again have any troubles with planks or with dogwalks. In fact, he grew to love them almost as much as the A-frame. It didn't matter how narrow they were, how they bounced, or what they were made of. He was used to the narrowness and the vibration. He knew where his back end was, and how to bounce a board. He had developed the skills he needed to have confidence with planks.

And as for me? I was at last beginning to understand the almost Zen-like state you need to get into if you really want to work as an animal trainer. You have to put aside your own desires—what it was that you meant to accomplish tonight, or in this training session, or even this year. You can have your goals, certainly—what is life without goals? But when you work with animals, especially sensitive or high-drive perfor-mance animals, you have to be prepared at any moment to put aside what you wanted to accomplish and work with what's ac-tually going on inside the animal's head. You have to be ready to attend, and to respond appropriately.

I still had a long way to go in my education as a dog trainer, but I was now much closer. I had begun to come to grips with a realization that I had avoided till now—that I had been a big part of the troubles we'd had. Me. Not Willow. I had to learn to put aside my own ambitions and plans, and deal with real-ity. It was a lesson I hadn't yet fully absorbed, and one I would have to learn again before we were through. And I was still a ways from understanding that any of this might be applicable to *humans*. Still, I was astonished and inspired by what I had been able to accomplish under Sue's tutelage with this yearling collie—who at times had looked so unpromising to me. It had thrilled me to watch Willow edge his great furry body out on that high dogwalk for the first time. And when I think today of how well he did that night, with barely enough training under his belt, a little piece of my heart is up there on that plank with him still.

IV. Goals

Twelve

I suppose it goes without saying that I felt pretty good after our success with the dogwalk. I was feeling pretty good about Willow, and, I have to say, pretty good about myself—although in retrospect I can see that I had very little to be proud of. Most of what we had accomplished was due mainly to Sue Reed's coaching, and to Willow's obliging nature, and to his doing his job. Still, my old desires and ambitions couldn't help but come roaring back. At this point, we had two weeks off from agility class before our new session with Cheryl Wells, and I decided that I should take the break as an opportunity to go and see what a real agility competition looked like—to see what we were striving toward.

These days I don't suppose for a moment it was a complete coincidence that the agility competition I chose to go and view was not just any old agility trial, but the Agility Nationals held the first weekend of November in Springfield, Massachusetts. I had heard about this upcoming event at our last agility class, and it was just too tempting not to go—though there were other, lower-level competitions I could have attended closer to home that would have been more typical trials, and certainly more appropriate to the level Willow and I were at. If I had dreamed of going to the "Dog Olympics," well this certainly was it in Springfield. The top dogs from around the country who had been competing on the agility circuit all year were converging that weekend on this small city in western Massachusetts, on the cluster of warehouses and exhibition halls that comprised the "Big-E" Exposition Center. The event would begin with the State Teams Competition on Friday, and then the individual events would be held on Saturday and Sunday. I didn't want to go alone, so I talked my husband into knocking off work on Friday to go with me and watch for a few hours while our son was in school—that way we wouldn't need to find a sitter. And so we dropped Daniel at school early Friday morning, and Steve and I set out for the two-hour drive west on the Mass Pike to Springfield.

I'm not quite sure what I was expecting to see. Any old agility match with nice doggies plodding slowly over their obstacles and wagging their tails? On some level, I must have appreciated that I was going to be seeing the absolute top dogs and handlers in the country—but somehow I still wasn't quite prepared. Perhaps I couldn't have been. Agility is a bit like horse racing or NASCAR. It is one of those lived experiences that you can't quite understand until you've been there, and even afterward, even when you know what it's like, you can't quite explain what you've seen. You can say that thoroughbreds are powerful, that there's nothing quite like standing and watching them from behind the white rail as they thunder by. You can even see them on TV. But you won't really see. You won't really understand—not until you've stood by the rail at Saratoga and had those powerful beasts blow past you mere inches from your nose with their unimaginable, heart-stopping speed. Felt the heated puffs of their breath balloon past your face as you stood there openmouthed, your cheeks spattered with flying mud.

Agility is like that at the highest levels. Only with dogs.

But how to describe it? It is difficult even today to create a single impression of what I saw. There were so many new things coming at me all at once. But I shall try.

To begin with, agility is a *race* against the clock. It is tremendously fast, a fact I hadn't yet focused on in our training. I think that, in our beginners class, we were so bent simply on mastering the individual obstacles, and on trying not to trip over our own feet or our dogs, that it hadn't yet sunk into my mind that once you figured out how to do it all, you were supposed to go *really, really fast*.

The competition was held in a large, echoing exhibition hall at the Big E, with two large rings marked out by low, flimsy-looking picket fences, and carpeted with bright green Astroturf. One ring was devoted to the larger dogs, and the other to the smaller dogs—and each of the rings was laid out with a standard agility course that included all of the familiar equipment we had seen in class: A-frame, dogwalk, pause box, tunnel, chute, weave poles, bar jumps, tire jumps; as well as a few pieces of apparatus we hadn't yet seen: the broad jump, and the "teeter" or seesaw. The two rings were surrounded by bleachers and folding chairs for the spectators, and there was a small, knowledgeable-looking crowd present. A short distance from the rings were a couple of concession stands selling hot dogs and drinks, and a few booths hawking agility equipment and training merchandise and all manner of dog cookies and treats. The air smelled strongly of popcorn and dog dander, and more faintly of manure and restroom. There was also, of course, the sound of barking—though surprisingly few dogs were actually present in the exhibition hall. It seemed that they were brought in from vans and SUVs parked outside just for the time that they were competing. And over the whole scene came the reverberating drone of the announcer calling the runs.

I took almost none of this in, at least not at first, for when Steve and I entered the hall, the dogs were already running, and all other perception fell away before their blinding speed. So fast were they that, the moment they began their runs, they seemed reduced to a black and white blur—for they were nearly all black and white border collies—yet somehow at the same time, they seemed almost to be moving in slow motion. It was that kind of speed. The kind of velocity that deceives the mind. The kind of speed with which the eye has trouble keeping up.

The dogs took turns rushing from obstacle to obstacle, jump, jump, teeter, tunnel, whoosh, ruddering with their tails on the turns, flattening out over jumps, their ears pressed flat to their heads. Their bodies took on a streamlined grace as they whisked about the floor, pumping with the same up and down motion you see dolphins using in the water. Words like "fleet" and "agile" don't begin to capture it. Weaving through the lines of vertical poles, their freckled collie noses drilled like high-speed sewing machines stabbing a zigzag pattern into a bobbin. They were vivid, blinding, stunning. Dice, Random, Jag, Chaos. Even their names sounded fast, as the announcer called them out one by one.

At this point I was standing behind the low picket fence encircling the big-dog ring with my husband, watching all of this, but having a bit of trouble seeing. Tears had sprung to my eyes as these brilliant dogs flashed past. They were so beautiful, so utterly amazing. I was crying for the sheer gorgeousness of their performance, for all the effort Willow and I had already put into this sport, for bitterness at my long lost Tippy who probably could have done this. For Willow, who would never be able to perform like this. Nobody had to tell me; I saw it in an instant. In a moment, I understood exactly what I had done—I had been trying to do a steeplechase with a Clydesdale; I had brought a pickup truck to Indy. Willow was already too big and heavy and slow. Even if I could learn how to be a decent handler (a big *if* at this point), he would never be anywhere near as fleet and lithe and agile as these border collies. He would never be able to do what they were doing in front of me right now, and certainly never with this heart-wrenching, breath-stealing speed, no matter how long and hard we trained.

My husband saw it too. "Wow," he said. "I guess poor old Willow will never be able to move that fast. Holy cow." He didn't add the further thought, but later driving home would say, "You know, if you really want to do agility, maybe you ought to get yourself a border collie." (That idea, of course, had already crossed my disloyal mind.)

There is a myth about agility—that you can do it with any old dog. That it's a fun game that anyone can play with the family pet. That certainly was the line I heard when I first started training Willow. I had read this in magazines, and was told as much at agility demos at dog shows. If you have a healthy pet dog—the line went—then sure you can do it. All you have to do is go out and try. On some level, this probably is true. Almost anyone can take the family dog to a beginner agility class and have fun trying to get him to walk a balance beam or shoot through a tunnel for cookies. But a dog must have a certain level of drive, talent, and willingness to take direction even to run a standard agility course within the requisite course time, even at a novice level. And the upper levels of the sport of agility are dominated almost entirely by just a few high-drive herding breeds, mainly border collies at the higher jump heights, and shelties at the lower jump heights. And many of the best dogs have been bred and selected specifically for the sport. That is what we saw at Springfield that day. These were not your common backyard pets. That is what you see at any high-level agility competition.

In retrospect, I'm not sure why this surprised me so. I should have known that the old breed and cull procedures for turning out working dogs had never actually gone out of fashion. The truth is that people who are serious about winning at dog and horse sports go to great lengths to acquire animals with loads of natural talent, drive, and speed. Often they end up breeding their own. You see this with thoroughbreds and greyhounds, with quarter horses and hunting dogs, with dogs used for sledding, herding, tracking, and retrieving. Even service and seeing-eye dog providers pretty much breed their own dogs. There is only so much that training can do. A lot of it is in the genes and hardwired into behavior. Or so I was beginning to see.

Once I had gotten my initial burst of emotion somewhat under control, my curiosity began to take over, and I began observing a bit more about this AKC agility competition that we were at—as Steve and I strolled around the two agility rings. There were two types of courses being used at the competition: The standard agility course, which was laid out with 15–20 obstacles in various configurations so as to require all sorts of quick turns, fancy jumping, and side changes by the handlers. There was also a kind of course called "Jumpers with Weaves." Here most of the agility equipment was removed—all except for the jumps, the weave poles, and a tunnel or two—in short, the really fast stuff was left in the ring—and things were laid out even more for speed. The Jumpers with Weaves course is a tremendously fast course—much faster than the standard agility course—and it truly becomes a blindingly fast steeplechase for dogs.

With both kinds of courses, the dogs were sorted into levels of achievement for their runs: Novice, Open, and Excellent A and B; and by the jump heights the dogs would be expected to jump. That day we saw dogs jumping at 8", 12", 16", 20" and 24", which are the standard jump heights for AKC agility, though in some venues there is also a 4" jump height for toy breeds. The dogs are basically expected to jump repeatedly at about the height of their shoulder.

At the higher jump heights we watched—the twenty- and twenty-four-inch divisions—things were, as I have already noted, dominated almost entirely by border collies. The other breeds of dog, when they appeared—the occasional golden retriever or the odd Portuguese water dog—looked rather slow and stupid by comparison, especially at the weave poles where the compulsive border collies seemed always to excel. On the other hand, the border collies were so supreme, they so utterly ruled the floor, that Steve and I found ourselves rooting for the other breeds who had accomplished so much even to enter the ring with those black and white rockets. I would later read somewhere that, in England—to deal with this issue—some venues hold what are called "ABC" events, meaning "Anything But Collies," where breeds of dog other than border collies get to compete against each other. In the United States, some breed clubs similarly hold "specialty events"—where only their own breeds are allowed to compete.

Steve and I mostly stood around the big dog ring watching the Standard Agility runs, but eventually there was a break while the Jumpers with Weaves course was set up, and we wandered over to take a look at the smaller dogs running in the other ring. At the sixteen-inch jump height, and to a lesser extent at twelve inches, the shelties and a few small border collies still dominated the competition. It was only at the lowest jump heights, of eight and twelve inches, that we saw any real diversity of breeds. There we did see a good smattering of shih tzus, corgis, mini-pins, and papillons. The smaller dogs were actually a lot more interesting to watch because of the assortment of breeds. Each breed, with its own unique conformation, had its own way of tackling the agility course, its own style and problems—the shih tzu looking like a flying mop, trying to see where it was going; the tiny papillon with its huge butterfly ears doing its best to press the great heavy teeter to the ground, and nearly having to hop up and down to do so.

It is still my observation today that the greatest variety of breeds, and the most fun, can be found in small dog agility, though one wonders how long it will be before the small agility breeds become as standardized as the larger ones. Lately, ominous signs have begun to appear. Some breeders have been producing a line of very fast, high-drive black and white papillons that look and act to my eye very much like tiny border collies. It seems that eventually this breed will come to dominate the lower jump heights just as the border collies and shelties now do at the higher heights. The sad fact is that an agility dog is like any other kind of performance animal. A Percheron is never going to best a quarter horse at the quarter horse's game. A golden retriever or a rough collie is never going to beat the average border collie at agility. It just isn't going to happen.

The good news about AKC agility—and this is something I hadn't quite focused on yet while we were in Springfield, but later would—is that while the other breeds certainly aren't going to wrest the highest levels of competition from the border collies—they can compete and gain titles. Under the AKC rules, a dog doesn't actually have to win the race and get the best time in order to earn what are called "legs" toward the various agility titles offered. The dog needs only complete the agility course without disqualifying mistakes and within the requisite course time in order to earn a "qualifying score" or a "Q." Now understand me here, this is still no small thing. It is an enormous and often insurmountable task for most breeds, and for most individual dogs. However, it is doable if you have a relatively fit, lithe animal that is willing to take direction.

That's why there are lots and lots of agility trials all around the country today with all sorts of breeds of dog running in them. These rules make agility accessible even to nonherding breeds, and these days a lot of purebred dog breeders—even those with relatively non-lithe breeds, such as bulldogs or Rottweilers—will at least attempt to put agility titles on their dogs in order to demonstrate that they are fit and capable. AKC agility competitions have become a way for breeders to prove that their dogs can still cut it. That they aren't just useless beauty queens. Of course, this is true for some purebred dogs and not for others—I will have more to say later on the subject of the overbreeding of purebred dogs, since it is an issue that came to afflict Willow and me. But I do think it is no coincidence that agility trials have become a fixture at many of the larger AKC conformation shows in this country.

Thirteen

On our way home from Springfield, I asked Steve to drive. I was still consumed with what I had seen at the agility nationals—I still had those stunning black and white border collies flashing about their courses in my mind as I tried to nap, my face cold against the car window. I'm not sure how much of my long-ago training with Tippy I had remembered until that moment, but it now all came flooding back upon me as the road rolled away under our car and my eyelids slid shut. I had once had one of those incredible, driven creatures myself, and she had brought me my early and only success as a dog trainer (or so I thought, bitterly, childishly). Having just been reminded of what a really high-drive working dog could do, I now wanted a BC of my own again with a sort of painful desire that bordered on lust.

Poor Willow, his every aspect was compared unfavorably in my mind against the standard of those fabulous border collies. He really was too big for agility, I thought, feeling at that moment rather sorry for him. His coat was too heavy, his legs a bit long. His paws were rather clumsy and floppy. He was sweet and biddable, but not sharp or acute. He had good drive for your average house pet, but nothing to compare with the laserlike focus of those BCs. He would never crouch that way to zip through the weave poles, or rocket about a course with the controlled speed of a guided missile. He liked to work, but he wasn't driven, compulsive, keen. (You will notice me here, forgetting how nasty and snappy those BCs back in agility class were.) Oh, why did I ever get a rough collie, a Lassie dog, I wondered, when what I really wanted was Tippy back? Sweet, talented, trembling little Tippy. Tippy would have been able to do this, I thought fiercely. *She* would have made a *great* agility dog.

There was silence in the car on the way home—except for Steve saying that line about maybe I ought to get myself a BC. He drove while I dozed and spun out lurid fantasies of success in my distressed brain. In some of my dreams, I had Tippy back, and we were blazing around an agility course before roaring crowds. In others, my new BC pup and I were running our first course with Sue Reed standing by and marveling that she'd never seen such a promising agility prospect. Ever. When I roused myself at a gas station, I saw Steve glance over at me once or twice. He said little, but he must have known what I was about. When we pulled up at Daniel's school to pick him up, our son bounced in the door asking excitedly, "So how was the dog show?" Steve shook his head and said, "We saw some pretty amazing border collies. They went really, really fast. Your mother may have to get one of those dogs if she truly wants to do agility."

Our seven-year-old's face lit up. "Really? We could get another dog?" He shouted this question.

Steve and I looked at each other. We hadn't thought that far ahead—to whether our house and yard could hold two dogs. We should have had that conversation before mentioning the possibility of another dog to Daniel. "Well, that or trade in Willow," Steve finished lamely, shooting me a glance and no doubt wondering, not for the first time, how serious I was about this agility thing.

Daniel was no fool. He saw immediately where this was going. A rosy tint of outrage spread to his cheeks, and he turned on me and let me have it. "What!" he cried. "You'd get rid of Willow because he's too *slow*? I suppose you're going to get rid of me because I'm bad at baseball!"

Steve and I both rushed to reassure Daniel that, no, of course not—We weren't going to get rid of either him or Willow, that we loved them both more than words could possibly describe, and that all members of the family were going to be kept and were not going anywhere. Still, I did feel that I'd been caught red-handed. Wasn't that *exactly* the sort of thing I'd been plotting the whole way back from Springfield? Was I really prepared to ditch poor Willow and replace him with the first BC puppy I could get my hands on? I felt a stab of remorse for my disloyalty to my sweet, hardworking collie.

To top things off, when we got back home, there of course was Willow, waiting patiently behind the door, desperately happy to see us after we'd been gone all day. Daniel tackled him in an enormous hug, hanging on to him and practically riding him, crooning over and over, "We love you, Willow. Don't worry. We aren't going to get rid of you." All the while shooting Steve and me dirty looks. Willow, who adores Daniel, rubbed his big furry body against my son and nibbled his front teeth up and down both his arms. This little scene reminded me of exactly why I'd gotten Willow in the first place, and not a BC.

As an adult, I had switched from border collies to rough collies precisely for the reason that high-drive BCs make lousy house pets. I had been blessed as a child with an especially sweet and tractable female border collie, but generally speaking border collies need to work all the time, and get into terrible trouble if left in the house or yard unattended for long periods, something most family pets have to regularly endure. Many BCs just don't know how to "shut it off," as they say. They can also be very snappy around children and other dogs, as I had seen at agility class, and are often aggressive with strangers.

Rough collies, on the other hand, while still an obliging herding breed, have a much more admirable mix of traits for a family pet. They are sweet, gregarious, and fun loving. They enjoy socializing with humans. They are not ferocious or snappy and, generally speaking, are completely trustworthy with children. They are large and provide a fair amount of protection for the yard or, in my case, for a smallish woman out walking in the woods alone, but they aren't sharp like the protective breeds, the Doberman or the German shepherd. You don't have to worry about them ripping someone's head off. They have good working drive and excellent trainability, but they also know how to switch it off and take a long nap. They are, in short, extremely nice pet dogs, so long as you don't mind the grooming that comes with them. You can, in fact, look at rough collies as something of a compromise: a border collie toned down for house, yard, and kid, and prettied up with that fancy coat.

This was what I had wanted when I got Willow—and what I'd previously had as an adult. The dog I'd had before Willow was Pooh, a sweet, beautiful, fun-loving female rough collie, who had kept me company during my long days of study at college and then in law school. She guarded my shabby student apartments and provided the necessary study breaks at local parks. With her friendly, outgoing nature and enchanting good looks, she charmed my series of roommates and eventually—when I met him—Steve. She was, throughout her life, brave and loyal, and on more than one occasion she chased off burglars trying to break in or aggressive people or animals on the street at night. She lived to the ripe old age of thirteen, and died in my arms of cancer, one of those great, great dogs that live on in your heart long after they are gone. It was this wonderful rough collie that Steve and I were trying to replicate when we got Willow. Daniel was a boisterous five-year-old at the time we decided "the family needed a dog." We had our hands full with parenthood, though, and the last thing we would have wanted was a high-drive border collie that would have required constant attention. I was prepared to put a fair amount of work into a puppy, into training it and taking it for walks, but Daniel came first. We needed a dog like Pooh—an animal with a calm, stable disposition, and one that was trainable and trustworthy with kids, and good protection for me when Steve had to travel out of town.

My main concern—and the thing that I told the breeders I was looking for at the time we got Willow—was sweetness of disposition. I had heard, you see, that some rough collies had gotten overbred, and had become high strung and snappy. I wanted to make sure we got a dog that could be trusted to play with my son and his boisterous friends. This dog would, above all, have to be a good family dog. If I mentioned agility to Willow's breeder at all—and I believe that I did, remembering back—it was as an afterthought. I think I must have remarked that I might like to try this new sport of agility I'd heard about with the puppy, and the breeder said something like, "Oh, that's interesting. Let me know how it goes." But athleticism and speed were not in any sense on the list of what I wanted or needed in a dog. What I wanted was sweetness and tractability. This I got. Willow was then, and remains today, as sweet and gentle as the day is long. He has always been just wonderful with children, and he loves Daniel to pieces.

I remember standing there that day when we returned from Springfield, and watching Daniel maul Willow the moment we were in the door, and feeling grateful to Willow for how wonderful he was with my exuberant son. Willow, at this point, was wiggling in Daniel's grasp, wagging his tail and crooning and giving little yelps of playful joy. (He was probably also asking to go out in the yard after being locked up in the house all day.) He was so sweet with my son, and so pretty. How could I ever have thought of getting rid of him? What was I thinking?

Since Willow needed a walk—and partly out of my own guilt and disloyalty—I took the two of us to our favorite walking spot, ten minutes away by car, to the wooded Norris Reservation in Norwell, Massachusetts. There we went for a long, companionable walk through the beautiful pine forests, traversing several ponds and streams, and ending up at a boathouse on the North River. The late fall weather had been overcast in the morning, but by afternoon the sky had cleared, leaving a gusty, sunny day in the forties, perfect for hiking, the tall pines creaking in the wind. As we walked, I was reminded at every turn of the communication that Willow and I had developed through agility—as he gazed back at me for instructions on which way to go, or checked to see if I was coming and then dashed ahead. Perhaps I was finally beginning to understand that the wonderful rapport we had built up between us was one of the main things of value that, in the end, we would take away from our agility training.

To reward Willow for being his sweet, tuned-in self, and for generally being a great dog, I took a little extra time and stopped at one of our favorite watering holes along the way. I sat down on a rock, and pulled my windbreaker close around me, and listened to the air roaring through the pines, while Willow plunged into the little creek nearby, wading up to his shoulders and lapping up the cold, tea-colored water with his long reddish pink tongue. When he looked like he was done drinking, I called him to me and pulled out a baggie of dog biscuits that I had brought along in my pocket. He came to me dripping water off his white leggings, crooning and wagging, and accepted his biscuits, which I broke up and fed to him in pieces. They smelled lovely. They were a healthy, organic dog biscuit made with bran, molasses, and cinnamon, which collided pleasantly with the gentle odor of wet dog in my nose. I must have been in a strange mood, for I found myself nibbling on one of the biscuits myself. They were fibrous and mildly sweet, and tasted like extremely healthy cardboard.

I can't account for this sudden taste for dog biscuits. I have almost never eaten pet food or dog biscuits in my life. Like most humans, I have a suspicion of any food product made for animals. On this day, though, perhaps I was trying to get myself back on Willow's wavelength, or at least trying to get back into the friendship and commonality we had shared—and how better to be companionable with friends than to share your trail food? In truth, though, I must also have been thinking of those BCs and feeling guilty for it.

Eventually a couple of people came along the trail—two middle-aged women who were walking along without a dog of their own. They caught sight of Willow, who always looks so lovely in the forest, especially in fall when the leaf and pine needle colors perfectly match his red-blond coat—and they had to make a fuss over him, as strangers always do. "Oh, my," they cried. "What a gorgeous collie! Just look at him, just like Lassie. Isn't he lovely? Oh, to have a dog like that! Aren't you the lucky one?"

Was I lucky? In my heart, I still wanted that BC puppy. I sat there blinking at the women for a moment, not saying anything. They gazed expectantly at me. Perhaps they wondered if I were deaf or slightly insane. Eventually I came to my senses and nodded graciously, the way dog owners do—as if I had any responsibility for the way Willow looked, other than occasionally brushing him.

"Yes," I said at last. "Well, yes. I guess I *am* lucky. He *is* lovely."

Fourteen

I wish I could say today that what turned me around, and off my obsession with border collies and back to training Willow, was some sense of love or loyalty to my dear sweet teammate who had worked so hard and so well for me in Sue Reed's agility class, especially mastering the dogwalk. But unfortunately, we humans—with our abstract plans and ambitions for the future—are often far less loyal than our poor dogs. If loyalty to Willow were all that was holding me back, then I must confess I probably would have dropped him in a heartbeat—even over the protests of my family—and gone straight out and started looking for that BC puppy. No, what prevented me was something else. It was, I think, a sense of my own shortcomings.

I had by now done enough agility training to have developed a rather keen sense of my own limitations and failings as a handler and trainer. I think that by now I understood I wasn't up to a really fast dog, not yet at any rate, not like those dogs we'd seen in Springfield. Perhaps I never would be. I could see by now how I reacted to the pressures of the moment, how I would get tangled up in my own limbs and would make mistakes, and get turned around on even the shortest courses we were running in class. There are some people who are good at sports. I have never been one of them. I will not bore you with tales of kicking the ball the wrong way in the big girls' soccer game back in high school. You will have to take my word for it. I was no good. Suffice to say that, even with my retained bitterness over losing Tippy, and my dreams of a really talented BC—a dog that could make me look better than I really was—I did appreciate with a sort of grim resignation that I wasn't yet up to a dog like that. I was so inexperienced and untalented as a handler that, even if I were to get such a dog, I wouldn't know what to do with it. The truth was, those BCs scared me. And, as I reviewed my own defects as a handler in the aftermath of the Springfield trial, I began to appreciate Willow on a completely new level. I began to see that—while he might not be the fastest or most agile dog on the planet—still, he was hardworking and biddable. He might not be my dream dog, but he very well might be the perfect dog to learn on. Also, I did have the developing sense that what I had just seen was the absolute top level of competition, and I knew somewhere in my brain from seeing those agility demos at dog shows that there were other, lower levels of competition where golden retrievers and springer spaniels and other breeds far slower than those missilelike BCs were somehow plodding through their agility courses. And earning titles.

As we approached the time to go back to agility class, it began to seem to me as if Willow ought to be afforded the same chance as those dogs—to take the sport as far as he could go. I wouldn't go so far as to call this *loyalty* to Willow exactly, more guilt or perhaps owing it to him. But I did feel that I should give him his best shot. He had worked for me so hard and so well that it seemed as if he had earned it. I no longer wanted or expected to win ribbons with him. That goal had gone out the window. Now I just wanted to compete, just to play the game. That seemed like a reasonable new goal given my own experience level and the talent of my dog. Willow would be the dog I would learn on. And then, I thought, if I continued to like the sport—*then* I would go out and get myself that BC puppy.

To compete—simply to play the game. It sounds like a small thing, a small goal, but now—having seen an actual agility competition—I began to get excited about going back to agility class. As our new training session came upon us, I began to get really enthused about competing, even if it was just at the novice level or at some routine and undistinguished venue—a fun match or a backyard "Show 'n Go." In a way, this new dream—this new goal—was both smaller and much more achievable than my previous pie in the sky ambitions. It is one thing to dream of being Tiger Woods and of playing golf in the Masters. Quite another thing to actually put yourself to the test and enter the local golf tournament at the country club down the road. Smaller, more realistic goals are, I now think, often more exciting and satisfying—because they are more reachable and manageable. They are something you actually *could do*, and really put yourself to the test. Having been given a big dose of reality, I had done what any reasonable human being would do—I had lowered my sights and set new goals that I had some reasonable prospect of achieving. And now, having done so—and simply wanting to compete—it all suddenly seemed quite possible in a way that it never really had before. In the end, seeing the Springfield trial proved for me as energizing as it was depressing—at least after the fact. Sure my dog was no BC, but he liked doing agility, he liked working with me, and it seemed as if eventually—with lots more training—we would be able to hack our way through a novice course, even if it wasn't a completely clean run or under course time. Hey, maybe we could even pick up a novice title. Was that too much to hope?

And so, as class drew near, I signed on the Internet and began ordering brochures with titles like, *Entering Your First Agility Trial.* We can compete! I thought. We can do this! I read about getting your dog measured for his first trial—to set his correct jump height. I read about finding trial listings, and sending in your "premium" (entry fee), and how you go about qualifying for titles. I read about scoring and judges and timers. About standard course times and faults and refusals and missed contacts. Having seen a real agility trial, the details suddenly seemed terribly interesting and exciting to me in a way they never had before. By the time we arrived at Cheryl Wells' agility class, I was fired up and ready to go, as was my dog. After two weeks off, Willow was positively itching to get back to agility. He barked like a mad beast as we pulled into the muddy parking lot outside the big blue equestrian arena. The potholes in the gravel were now beginning to ice over as winter approached, and the crisp frigid night air seemed to hold for us both a renewed vigor and resolve—now that we had more concrete goals in mind.

When I look back on all of this now, it seems almost comical to me how frequently and radically my goals for this sport changed. At first I had no goals or ambitions at all, either for myself or my dog. I was just out to give the sport a try. Then, as Willow began to look promising one moment, and dismally untalented the next, it was as if my mind were being whipsawed about, foolishly dreaming of glory one moment and of quitting the sport for good the next.

I think that, as a result of my agility experience, I have come to see goals in a different light. I used to think of them as external, fixed objects. As a sort of ideal that you would strive or crane toward, whether or not you ever reached them. Today, I see goals very differently, as stretchy, flexible things—like rubber bands or underwear. You try them on to see how they fit. And when they grow too large or too small, you throw them away, simply dispense with them. They are, in the end, quite disposable. Really, who needs them? They were just something you dreamed up for yourself in the first place.

V. Theory

Fifteen

Cheryl Wells, our new instructor and Sue Reed's protégée, was a stocky athletic young woman with cropped honey-blond hair and a freckled nose, and an air about her of the tomboy. She strode about the sawdust floor of the horse arena, her muscular thighs pumping, running us through our drills—and as she did so, she reminded me of the girls I used to play soccer with in high school. She had that same falsely self-deprecating manner of the true sports perfectionist, shrugging and mugging as if with modesty, yet holding herself to an excruciatingly high standard. Her own dog, Jett, was one of those fleet black and white border collies we had seen out in Springfield. Someone like Cheryl would never have anything else. When Jett was off leash, this dog would drill through the weave poles just for fun with that same zigzag action we had seen at nationals. I recognized what I was seeing and felt a stab of jealousy. It didn't help that Jett was a small blue-black female who looked a lot like Tippy. When not working, Jett was deeply intense, standing crouched beside Cheryl, braced for her next command. Jett was also rather snappy and fearful around other dogs, and so during class Cheryl left her tied to a wall of the arena and told us to keep our own dogs' noses away from her. Another dog would have dozed off, but not Jett. She could watch Cheryl for hours, her attention never flagging, studying her every move.

Willow, for his part, had gone from being the dunce of the beginners' class to the star. There was a brand new set of recruits for this class, new dogs and new handlers, most of whom had never done agility training before—the rest of our old, more experienced class (including our friend the Rottweiler) having either been promoted to advanced beginners or having dropped out along the way. This shift of ranks benefitted Willow, for—suddenly—*he* was the most experienced dog in the class, and he had by now mastered nearly everything that he would be asked to do at the beginners level. For once, he was best at everything, prancing across planks, whipping through tunnels, stepping through ladders with a bit of wiggle in his now educated butt. (*He* knew where *his* back paws were, thank you.) He loved being top dog, and often got to be Cheryl's "demo dog"—to show the other dogs what to do.

One night, Cheryl used Willow to demonstrate "targeting." In our previous classes with Sue Reed, we had been taught how to get our dogs to touch their noses to a white plastic disposable coffee cup lid. The lid was the "target," which could then be placed wherever you wanted the dog to go. Once a dog had learned, *"go target,"* you could place the lid behind a jump, for example, and the dog would take the jump to touch the target. There are many uses for targeting in agility; this is just one. In Sue Reed's class, we had mainly been using targets as something to aim for when jumping through the doughnutlike tire jump. Willow had long since mastered "going out" (or going away from me) to touch the target. I had spent some time training him for this at home, starting with the target/

lid stationary on the ground near us and rewarding him just for touching it with his nose. Gradually, at Sue's instruction, I moved the lid farther and farther out until I had Willow trotting happily back and forth between me and the target, which often was up to twenty feet away. Eventually, this turned into a good game for us. I began holding the white plastic lid in my hand and pitching it out as far as I could, like a Frisbee. Coffee cup lids are not great flyers, and our lid would always careen off in unpredictable directions and at uncertain speeds. Willow liked the target even better when it was in motion, and he had great fun chasing it down and pouncing on it as if it were a small fleeing animal. This was where things stood the night of Cheryl's targeting demonstration with Willow.

At this particular class, the target was being used for a new purpose—to slow the dogs down as they came flying off the A-frame. There is a yellow "contact zone" painted across the bottom of the A-frame that the dogs must touch with their feet in order to perform the obstacle correctly. This is mostly a safety requirement. You don't want a dog leaping off the top of the high A-frame because he might get hurt. So the dog is required to touch this yellow zone at the bottom of the obstacle in order to assure that he actually *climbs down* the far side, and doesn't leap off. He needs only to get one paw in the zone, but this requires him to put on the brakes and slow himself as he comes zipping off the far side of the A-frame—not always an easy thing to do, especially if the dog is large and moving fast. One way to train a dog to slow down is to teach him to keep his head low as he descends the steep slope of the A-frame. This is where the coffee cup lid comes in. If the dog is bent on touching a target on the ground, then he automatically lowers his head and brakes his speed as he comes off the A-frame.

At our first and second classes, Cheryl had taught all of the dogs to perform a low A-frame. Then, on this night, she placed the white plastic coffee cup lid on the ground right where the dogs would come off the A-frame. We then sent Willow over the A-frame as the "demo dog" and commanded him to—"*go target*"—as he came down the far side. Willow hadn't done this exercise before, but he knew his targets. He spotted the coffee cup lid as he came over the apex of the A-frame, lowered his head, put on the brakes, half slid down the far side of the A-frame digging in his toenails, and hit the yellow contact zone perfectly, nudging the white plastic lid with his nose as he went by—then looked around for his cookie. "Oohs" and "Aahs" went up from the class. To the newbies in the class, I realized, Willow looked incredibly well trained and knowledgeable. Several of our new classmates said things like, "Wow, Willow's really good," shaking their heads, or "How did you get him to do that?" a note of amazement in their voices.

If only they knew, I thought. To them it still looked like magic.

Of course, by this time I knew very well that there was no conjuration involved. It was a matter of practice, practice, practice; of having a willing, motivated dog; and of breaking things down into small manageable parts that could be easily trained: Chase the target for fun. Low, low A-frame and big handfuls of meat. Move the target out a little further, and then after a while start putting obstacles in the way. Later, when the whole thing came together, it truly did look rather stunning—especially if you hadn't seen the hours of tedious work that went into producing the behavior chain.

These days, when I flick on Animal Planet at night and see some dog perform a series of amazing tricks—such as run an obstacle course with an egg in his mouth, then dive into a pool, swim across, and deliver the egg unbroken into his handler's hand—I immediately start breaking down in my head how you'd train all that stuff. The dive into the pool could clearly be taught separately. You'd want to begin the egg carry with a small ball, maybe a golf ball. And you might want to use a retriever for this task—a dog with a love of water and a naturally soft mouth. You probably wouldn't get far training a husky to carry that egg. Finding a dog with native talent. Breaking the task down into small manageable steps. You see these same themes over and over in dog training.

Our new class moved terribly slowly, with a whole bunch of new dogs being introduced to the agility equipment for the first time. I didn't mind. Having been through this before, I knew that things would quickly speed up, and soon we would be running drills through combinations of obstacles. And Willow was getting what he needed—he was having the chance to show off his tricks and build his confidence.

The other thing that made this repeat class worthwhile for us was that Cheryl—in her self-deprecating way—was a far more technical teacher than Sue Reed. It's funny; you wouldn't think she would be. She was far more unassuming and less authoritarian in her manner than Sue, with her shrugging smiles and informal ways. But that perfectionism of hers would kick in, and by the second or third class she was throwing around a lot of training jargon and bringing out handfuls of clickers. Unlike Sue, she made it clear that we would be expected to use them.

Now that she had demonstrated one of the uses of targeting, Cheryl said that she was going to show everyone how to teach their own dogs targeting, and we were going to do it using our new clickers. "What, you don't have one? Here—use this one, and you can pay me for it after class. That'll be $2.50. Or pay me next time."

And so I suddenly found myself standing there in class, blinking with surprise, and holding in my hand the cool plastic of my own new little clicker—rather, I must say, against my will. I don't think I had realized until that moment that I had been resisting the whole idea of clickers.

You may recall that previously I had run into the concept of clickers back in my early Web searches, and had discussed with Sue Reed whether I should be using one in training Willow. When Sue had said I didn't have to use one, I had taken this as, *No don't bother*, or *No, you don't need one*. However, it wasn't as if Sue had forbidden the use of clickers in her class. In fact, she had made clear that you could use one if you wanted to, and that a clicker could be a very useful training tool. And I had seen some of the more experienced handlers occasionally using one in class. The truth is, I had no interest in learning to use a clicker, and had been happy to be let off the hook. I don't need one of those things, I had thought. *Nope. No thanks. Not for me.*

It's a little hard for me today to understand why I was so resistant to the whole idea of using a clicker, when I now know what an incredibly useful device it can be, and how utterly indispensable in teaching certain tasks. I think that some of my trouble was a natural human aversion to anything new or foreign. Sure, I had given up my old choke collar, and I could see that the positive training methods worked better, but the clicker still seemed strange and unfamiliar—part of a program I wasn't quite getting with yet. Also, clickers seemed at the time, frankly, a bit gimmicky or new-agey, like snapping your wrist with a rubber band to quit smoking, or taking a placebo pill.

Have you seen one of these things? They sell them at most pet and toy stores these days, and they have found application in everything from animal training to business management to socializing autistic children. A clicker basically consists of a small strip of flexible aluminum or some other metal alloy mounted on a toggle inside a rectangular plastic housing, so that the metal strip can be depressed with the thumb, making a hollow metallic "click-click" sound. The whole assembly is about the size of a matchbox, and has the light, cheap feel of a toy from a fast-food drive-through window. What I discounted at this point was that the "click-click" wasn't just a mental gimmick, but could be used very effectively as a signaling device.

At any rate, I found myself standing there in Cheryl's class, gazing skeptically at the clicker in my hand, and wanting rather pigheadedly to resist it. My clicker was formed from orange and baby blue molded plastic, and the metal strip inside made a sort of *sproing* sound, instead of a solid *click-click*. Fortunately, I didn't have a lot of time to throw up mental barriers because here was Cheryl, moving right along and telling us to gather round her.

She started by doing a demonstration with one of the new and completely uninitiated dogs in the class. The dog she picked was an incorrigible little wheat colored terrier named Gizmo. This dog was about the size and shape of a mailbox, and appeared not to have had much training. I say this because he wasn't doing sits or offering paw the minute the treats came out, the way most dogs with even a little training will. He was just jumping around at the end of his leash like the silly little dog that he was. Today, having more or less mastered the art of clicker training, I know that Cheryl picked a lively little dog like Gizmo because an active dog—while harder to control—is easier to clicker train. This is because he will try things for you that you can then "mark" with the click, and reward. A more reserved dog like Willow might just stand there looking at you and waiting for instructions.

So here was Cheryl. She had a bag of treats on her belt, a clicker dangling from her left wrist by what looked like a short curly phone cord, a white plastic coffee cup lid in her right hand—and this crazy little dog jumping around in front of her. She took Gizmo by the leash, and immediately he started jumping up on her knees for treats, his bright beady eyes on her face, his body wriggling. Cheryl smiled at the dog and clicked the clicker—*click-click*—then handed him a treat. Gizmo was now jumping around with excitement, having swallowed the treat with lightning speed. Cheryl clicked again, and then again, each time giving the dog a treat. "What I'm doing right now," she said, "is just getting the dog used to the idea that a click means *the treat is coming*. That's what the click means to the dog. *A treat is coming.*" She paused to look around at the class. "I'm *conditioning* the dog," she said.

Conditioning. My mind balked at that word.

I never took any psychology courses at college, but this sounded a lot like what some of my roommates did back at Brown, with rats and Rice Krispies in Psych 101. I didn't exactly know what Cheryl was talking about, but with my legal and writing backgrounds, I usually detect when a word is being used in a new or unfamiliar way. The association I previously had with the word *conditioning* had to do with Pavlov and with drooling dogs. So was the clicker supposed to be making this little dog drool for treats? It seemed like Cheryl was saying something else. *Hmmm.*

"Okay," Cheryl said. "Now that Gizmo is conditioned to the click, I'm going to start *shaping* his behavior." *Shaping.* The way she said it, I could tell that this word, too, was a term of art that I was supposed to be paying attention to, a word freighted with theory I didn't fully understand.

"*Shaping*," Cheryl repeated and flipped the coffee cup lid through the air. It zinged past Gizmo's nose and landed on the ground two or three feet away from him. The little terrier looked momentarily confused, crossing his eyes to look at the end of his own nose where the lid had just gone flying past. Then he did what any dog would do. He went over to the coffee cup lid where it had landed, and sniffed at it. The minute the black dot of his nose came near the lid, Cheryl clicked and gave him a treat.

Gizmo was now focused on her and the treats again, and no longer on the lid. He jumped up on Cheryl's knees, pawed at her thighs, jumped a little to sniff the clicker. Cheryl stood impassive, waiting. After a while, the terrier lost interest in her and started nosing the ground again, looking for dropped treats. When his nose came near the plastic lid again—near it but not on it—Cheryl clicked him. The dog dove for the treat in her hand, by now having figured out what the click meant. *Cookies!* They repeated this same ritual several times before the dog seemed to realize that it was when his nose got near the plastic lid that the click happened. Eventually his nose actually brushed the lid, and Cheryl clicked and jackpotted him with a handful of treats. The terrier immediately went back to the lid and touched it again, earning more treats. You could almost see the lightbulb going on in the cartoon balloon over his small wiry head. Now it went quickly: touch the lid, get a click-treat, touch the lid, get a click-treat. They did this two or three more times, and then Cheryl said, "Okay, he's got it." This had taken all of maybe five or six minutes.

Cheryl turned to the rest of the class and said, "Okay, now the target *you* are all going to use is *your hand*."

Our hands? We handlers all examined our hands as if they were strange outer space objects. Cheryl saw our confusion. "Here," she said, "I'll show you." She went over and got her own dog, Jett, where she was tied to the wall, and brought her over to a jump. Cheryl held out her hand in front of Jett's nose and wiggled it a little. Jett knew this game well and followed Cheryl's hand as she moved it in a circle around the jump. Then Cheryl passed her hand across the jump, and Jett followed it, leaping over the jump. Cheryl's hand reversed direction, and Jett did, too, jumping back over the jump in the opposite direction. "You can see," Cheryl said, "that this can be a very helpful technique in guiding your dog through an agility course." She swept her hand through the air toward a tunnel, and Jett dove into it. Cheryl re-called her dog, and returned her to her tie-rope, then came back to us.

"Now you do it," she told us. "Get your dog to follow your hand. First *condition* your dog to the click/treat. Then teach your hand as a target, just as I did with Gizmo. Remember, we are *shaping* the behavior." *Conditioning, shaping.* There were those words again. "The dog doesn't have to be perfect," Cheryl said. "If he gets his nose near your hand, you can click that. Reinforce whatever is close to what you want." *Reinforce.* Now there was a word that I thought I understood, since Sue Reed had used that term more or less interchangeably with the word *reward*—but by now there was so much jargon flying around that I wasn't even sure I understood that word anymore. *More jargon*, I thought. *Ugh.*

I looked down at Willow and fondled my little orange and blue clicker. I felt rather apprehensive because it seemed as if I really didn't know what I was doing with this clicker training stuff. It all still looked to me like "reward the correct behavior." I couldn't see what the clicker was adding to the mix. *Still, what the hell*, I thought. *Here goes.* I depressed the thumbplate of my clicker, and it made a couple of metallic popping noises. *Sproing. Poing.* Willow's ears swiveled toward the sound. *Mom is making a weird noise. Why?* I handed him a treat. Then I clicked again. Again, treat. Willow's tail wagged. Okay, now he liked this noise. When I had done this five or six times, I stopped and looked around. Some of the other handlers had moved on to the hand/target thing. Willow nuzzled the clicker. He hadn't had his dinner yet tonight and was hungry, and he was starting to like this game because it was producing food. Okay, I thought, why not? I held out my hand a few feet from Willow's nose. This was the same hand that had been liberally dispensing treats, so of course Willow immediately nosed it. When his black spongy nose touched my hand, I depressed the clicker with my other hand, *sproing,* and gave him a treat. We did this a few more times, but it almost seemed too easy. Willow quickly caught on to the idea of *touch the hand, get a click-treat.*

All right, I thought, let's make this a little harder. I swept my hand through the air, away from Willow's nose, taking a couple of steps. Willow stood still, watching my hand move away from him. I wiggled my hand. He trotted over and nuzzled it again, and got another click-treat. I kept moving my hand around, and he trotted after it. *Click-treat. Click-treat.* Soon I was swooping my hand around in big arcs, and Willow was diving for it, dashing forward and thrusting his long sharp collie snout through the air to touch the flying hand.

In a short time, my steps had lengthened, and we were moving about the floor of the arena in a kind of rhythmic dance, with me making big sweeping strides and swinging my arm this way and that, traversing the sawdust floor in what must have looked like a kind of waltz. Swinging first to the right, and then the left, Willow following my every move, swirling around my legs, his big fluffy collie tail swishing about my knees like the ruffled hem of a dress. We swished and swayed and glided about, and for a moment time was lost. I was dancing with my dog.

After a while, I recaptured myself and looked up, and all around the arena all of the other dogs and their handlers were doing this, too. Sixteen of us—eight dogs and eight humans, all sweeping and swirling about the arena in long beautiful arcs, our hands held out in what looked almost like a formal pose from some nineteenth-century dance. Our dogs' tails swirled and swooshed about our legs, and the strains of the *Blue Danube* waltz came into my head. *One-two-three, one-two-three.*

On the way home from class that night, I felt a bit like Audrey Hepburn singing *I could have danced all night*, or Cinderella having returned from the ball with a canine Prince Charming. That, at least, was how I felt with the happy giddy charmed part of my brain. But by the next morning, one of those blustery grey late-fall mornings in New England, the slightly cranky, sleep-deprived part of my mind had taken over.

Okay, I thought, so Cheryl was able to pull off one of those bits of animal trainer sorcery last night. She gave us something to do with our dogs that was silly and fun and more magical than I possibly could have guessed—but now I wanted to understand how she had pulled it off using that little clicker. I still had words like *shaping* and *conditioning* and *reinforcement* going around in my head, and still no real understanding to back them up.

Along with my new clicker, I had brought home from agility class a small yellow brochure about clicker training. Once Daniel was off to school, I pulled my clicker and this skinny paperback out of the two-handled tote I took to agility class, and slouched down in an armchair in the living room still in my pajamas—yoga pants and a T-shirt. Scowling slightly, I poured over the brochure as I drank my third cup of coffee. The bright yellow brochure, while cheerful and instructive, was no more illuminating than Cheryl's class had been, but fortunately it had one of those nice "For More Information" sections at the back, listing a number of books and websites. The name Karen Pryor kept cropping up and her books were listed, and so at this point I sat down at my computer, signed on to Amazon, and ordered *Lads Before the Wind* and *Don't Shoot the Dog*. I didn't know it yet, but when these books came in the mail a few days later, they would finally provide me with the thinking behind what I had been doing since I signed up with Sue Reed back in September.

Sixteen

It was actually a good time for me to be introduced to the theory behind all of this agility training. I have since come to appreciate that it is difficult to absorb the teaching of abstract concepts until you are actually engaged in an activity. You may pick up a few things at the beginning. A little instruction up front can help you feel more comfortable getting started, but most of the subtleties will be lost on you until you are actually doing the thing you are trying to master. Now, though, with a little training under my belt, I was ripe to absorb the theory.

When Karen Pryor's books arrived in the mail, they didn't look too daunting. Both were paperbacks. *Don't Shoot the Dog!* had the look of a thin instructional manual for "dummies," the theory broken down into easy chapters with large headings followed by simple charts setting forth "approaches" to train "specific behaviors." I actually started reading with the other, fatter book, *Lads Before the Wind*. Some of this was avoidance. I still wasn't quite mentally ready to start with the dog training stuff, at least not right away. And *Lads* looked like the more interesting book. It was formatted more like a memoir and had the enticing subtitle *"Diary of a Dolphin Trainer."* Once I started reading, I was completely hooked by Pryor's conversational writing style and her delightful anecdotes about training marine mammals. Since I had been doing dog training myself, it was doubly fascinating to read the account of an experienced animal trainer who had worked with many different kinds of animals over the years.

By the time I was finished with *Lads*, I was avid to read even the dull-looking dog training manual, which turned out to be much better than it had first appeared. Pryor was uniquely qualified to explain clicker training theory, having a foot in both animal training and in science. The scientific and animal training camps don't usually have much to do with each other—each regarding the other as rather useless. To scientists, animal trainers look superstitious, unscientific, and anecdotal. To animal trainers, scientists appear as if they are willfully ignoring obvious signals from the animals, such as their evident emotional states. (For a long time, scientists refused even to countenance the idea that animals might *have* emotions.) Pryor, though, had started as an animal trainer married to a research scientist who was putting on marine mammal shows to support his research activities. She then worked as an animal trainer alongside scientists and being advised by them, and ultimately did some of her own independent behavioral research spurred by her training activities. So she had cred with both camps, and was able to bring together the two bodies of knowledge in her writing—for the first time attempting to explain why various training methods did and did not work.

Pryor's books finally laid out for me what it was I was supposed to be doing in Cheryl Wells' class. Operant conditioning,[4] Pryor

---

4. In this chapter, I am using words such as *reinforcement*, *operant conditioning*, *shaping*, *extinction burst*, and the like, in the senses that those words were taught to me in agility training, and as used by Karen Pryor in her books. Please note, however, that agility trainers do not necessarily use

explained, was different from classical or Pavlovian conditioning, which is a process whereby a stimulus is paired with a reward without regard to the animal's own efforts—for example, when a dog drools in response to a ringing bell because he knows the bell means his dinner's coming. In operant conditioning, by contrast, the animal learns to produce a desired result through the reinforcement of his *own* actions. So, for instance, a rat might learn to obtain a Rice Krispy by pushing a lever. The control is in the rat's own paws. He is "conditioned" to do the behavior—push the lever—because he learns that doing so will result in a reward, what is called a "positive reinforcer."

According to Pryor, operant conditioning was developed out of the behaviorism of B.F. Skinner. Skinnerian behaviorists, she said, basically treated animals like black boxes producing behaviors. They eschewed considering anything going on "subjectively" in the animal's head. They simply asked how a particular stimulus affected the animal's behavior. A "positive reinforcer" was anything that made it *more likely* that a particular behavior would occur. An "aversive" (sometimes called a "negative reinforcer"[5]) was anything that made it *less likely* that the behavior would occur. So if a rat pushes a lever and gets

these terms today in exactly the same way as they are used in contemporary psychology, or in the behaviorism that first inspired positive training theory. Positive animal trainers have, by now, worked out their own theories and ideas about how to train and communicate with animals, and so-called "operant" training theory should, in my opinion, be treated as a separate body of knowledge at this point, rather than trying to fit it into existing paradigms.

5.   I shall try to avoid using the term "negative reinforcement" because it is confusing. Some trainers use "negative reinforcement" to mean an aversive stimulus, while others use it to mean the reinforcement of a behavior through the avoidance of an aversive stimulus, such as when a horse turns its head to avoid pressure on the reins.

a Rice Krispy, he's more likely to push the lever again. That's a positive reinforcer. If the rat gets a shock, he's less likely to push the lever again. That's an aversive stimulus.

This all sounds pretty simple, but of course, when you apply these rules, you can't really treat animals like black boxes. It helps a whole lot to have some knowledge of the animal you're working with so that you know what the animal likes and dislikes. On the likes end, food is usually a safe bet. Most animals like their kibble quite a lot. However, there are some retrievers who like tennis balls better than food. And some animals just aren't terribly food motivated. Reinforcers will vary by species: a stinky half-rotted fish might look pretty good to a dog or a dolphin, whereas most people would find it repulsive. As a trainer, you have to figure out what motivates your particular animal.

Assuming that you can figure out what a good reinforcer is for your animal, the rule that has proven so very powerful for animal trainers is this: A behavior can be encouraged and intensified with positive reinforcement. A puppy who gets a tasty treat when he "comes" to you is much more likely to come— no, run!—to you; much more likely, that is, than if he gets a swat on the rump when he reaches you, possibly for not coming fast enough. Being swatted is actually a pretty strong aversive stimulus and will quickly encourage the puppy never to come. In her books, Pryor claimed that virtually any animal could be trained so long as you could "figure out how to reinforce it effectively and think of something interesting and appropriate for it to do." And this wasn't even limited to mammals. In *Lads*, Pryor told stories of trained pigeons and guppies, and even of a scallop taught to clap its shell for its dinner.

In addition to finding a good positive reinforcer for your animal, the other problem you run into in actually training animals is that you can't positively or negatively influence a behavior that isn't already occurring. So somehow you need to lure or cajole the animal into doing the behavior you want, or wait for it to happen naturally, so that you can reinforce it. I had seen this trouble with Willow and the plank when we started our agility training. I had wanted to reinforce him for getting up on the plank, but I couldn't jackpot him until I could actually get him up there. That was why we were spending a lot of time, especially early on, luring the dogs into doing things with extremely yummy treats. That or waiting for them to try things. We were trying to get them to perform behaviors that we could then reinforce.

Whether positive or aversive, the reinforcer must—as I had seen in Sue's class—occur in conjunction with the behavior so that the animal will associate the reward or punishment with the action. That's why timing is so crucial. If the corn comes too late after the chicken pulls the lever, the chicken won't associate pulling the lever with the food prize. However, as I had also found out in training Willow, it isn't always easy to be there with the treat at exactly the right moment in the midst of a training exercise.

This is where the introduction of a "marker" or "conditioned reinforcer" comes in, such as a clicker or a whistle, or—as Sue Reed would say—a sharp happy vocal signal *("Good!" "Yes!")*. What the signal means to the dog is, *"Good dog, you just won the treat!"* Once the dog is accustomed to working with the clicker, it also comes to mean, *"Yes, do exactly that. Right there. That's what I wanted."* As the trainer, you still have to supply the treat, but it becomes the timing of the click that's important, not the timing of the treat.

I found the mere fact of this quite liberating, once I got used to my clicker, because I was no longer having to wrestle a treat from my pocket or treat bag under such time pressure. Once I had clicked what I wanted Willow to do, I could then relax and deliver his treat at my leisure. It was the split-second timing of the clicker that made it such a valuable training tool.

Clickers also have the added benefit of encouraging the animal to be more involved in its own training, and to become more communicative in its own right. Once the animal knows that it's "working for the click," it will begin trying different things to "earn the click" (and therefore the treat). When you are working with a click-savvy dog, it's almost as if the dog is saying, *How's this? Is this it? How about this way?* Clicker training thus becomes a two-way communication loop, with the animal thinking up things to try, and you clicking precisely what you want.

I had my first experience with this teaching Willow to heel. Heeling was one of those things Willow and I had practiced for months and months in Puppy-K class, but we had never really gotten very good at it using a choke collar and leash. Willow knew that he was being choked and punished, but he never quite seemed to understand what for. I was starting to appreciate that he was a fairly sensitive dog, and that he hated being punished for no reason. Karen Pryor said, though, that heeling was one of the training tasks especially suited to teaching with a clicker, and so—after reading her books—it was one of the first things I decided to train with a clicker, since it promised to be a far gentler teaching method.

I started as *Don't Shoot the Dog* counseled, with Willow walking on a loose leash at my left side as we walked slowly around our backyard. Pryor said that what you wanted to do was to click the dog each time he got near the sweet spot—the place where you wanted him to be walking at your left heel. Like Cheryl teaching targeting, Pryor said not to expect perfection from your dog, just reward him each time he got close to the right spot. You could then gradually raise your expectations as the dog got used to the drill. This process of gradually raising the bar until you had what you wanted she termed "successive approximation."

In practice, I found clicker training the heel to be an extremely flexible and forgiving process. I could let Willow stray all around my left side as we walked, no worries, no stress, and then each time he got near my left hip, I'd click and treat him. The first few times this happened more or less by accident, but soon Willow caught on and began actively searching for the spot where I wanted him—a huge step forward. He seemed to be saying, *Here boss? Or right here?* You could see him shifting his weight around on his feet, trying out different positions, hesitating and then adjusting himself forward or backward with a jog of his hip and a swish of his tail. And listening all the while intently for that click, telling him, *Yes, right there.*

It was, I found, quite thrilling to be suddenly communicating so precisely with my dog—I who had always dreamed of such a private Morse code. It was as if I were suddenly speaking Willow's language. And, even more exciting, as if he could suddenly answer back—by showing me things. *Is this right? How about this?* As I have noted, animals communicate mostly nonverbally, and dogs are especially acute about the nuances of physical movement and body positions in space, and that was exactly the sort of thing that Willow and I were now "discussing" through the signaling device of our little clicker. Clickers are actually finely calibrated for teaching dogs refined maneuvers entailing specific body positions, such as heeling or jumping. It is the clicker's precision that makes this kind of communication possible, and—for dogs—very much on their own terms.

Willow, too, seemed to find the whole experience quite exciting, and to be avid for it. Once he had found the sweet spot at my side that he was aiming for, I began making things harder, speeding up, dashing forward, and then slowing down. It was incredible to see how quickly he was hugging my hip as I turned tight circles, first in one direction, and then the other, or slowed to the pace of a snail, at which point he would lift his paws slowly, like a dressage horse, and creep forward with me. He was, in short, fully engaged.

How different this was from the choke collar heeling we had done, where he was placed in a position and then choked for moving out of that position. I could see now that much of the difference in the two training methods lay in what was expected of the student/dog. With the old choke collar method, perfection was expected before the student (Willow) had ever even had a chance to learn anything, which seemed almost to assure my having to punish him. With the new clicker method, he could fail without consequence, yet was rewarded for each slight improvement. And each increase in my requirements actually seemed to excite him. In fact, I began to notice that if I *didn't* raise my criteria and make things harder—then he would start to get bored and lose interest in the game. He'd start to walk away, sniff the bushes.

It was at this point that I had to begin applying what Pryor termed "variable reinforcement" in order to hold his attention upon the task of heeling—for heeling is, in truth, a rather dull activity. What you do with variable reinforcement is this: in order to maintain at peak level a behavior the dog has already learned—you begin *not* to reinforce it *all the time*, but rather to give treats only *occasionally*, on a random reward schedule, varying the frequency of the treats. This has the unexpected effect of actually keeping the dog's interest.

This has always seemed counterintuitive to me. Why would a dog work better for fewer treats?

Exactly why variable reinforcement works is still something of a mystery to me, but I have heard the effect explained by trainers as being a bit like gambling. Karen Pryor talks about this in her books. It wouldn't be very interesting, she points out, if every time you put a nickel in a slot machine you reliably got out a dime. That game would quickly become predictable and boring, and you would stop playing. It's far more fun and exciting to put a bunch of nickels in the slot machine one by one, never knowing when suddenly you are going to get a huge payoff. Variable reinforcement is like that for animals. It's the gamble that keeps things interesting. The hard part for a trainer is in keeping the reward pattern truly random. It's easy to fall into a pattern of every third time or every fourth time. Animals are very smart about patterns, and as soon as one appears, they tend to lose interest. They have figured out the game. In practice, I've found with Willow that it helps to change up treats, sometimes providing a dull but nutritious biscuit, at other times a luscious piece of meat. Anything to throw off his expectations.

There is another aspect of withholding reinforcement that animal trainers also use to enhance performance. It's called the "extinction burst." An extinction burst occurs in classical psychology when you stop rewarding a behavior that previously had been reinforced. In this case, the behavior often will intensify before it goes away or is "extinguished." The example that is usually given is that of a child who is "rewarded" with a cookie when he whines. Eventually the parent realizes that the cookies are only making matters worse, and he or she wisely stops reinforcing the whining behavior with cookies. However, once the cookies stop coming, there is always a period during which "things get worse before they get better." The whining intensifies before it goes away. This is referred to as the "extinction burst"—the intensification of the behavior (the whining) before the child stops whining for cookies because the behavior is no longer being reinforced (extinction).

What animal trainers have been able to do is to tap into this "extinction burst" for higher or more novel performance. To do this, they focus upon the frustrated energy generated by the animal during the extinction burst phase. The example dog trainers I've worked with like to use is that of shaking a pen that's low on ink. If you try the pen and the ink doesn't come out the first time, you shake the pen, and the ink comes, and you write with it. However, if you were to shake the pen and the ink still didn't come, then you might then shake the pen again really hard one more time *in frustration* before you quit using it and threw it out. That last really hard shake is what interests animal trainers (and is what they are talking about when they say they are "using the extinction burst"). What is of particular interest to operant trainers is the *extra effort* and the *experimental wildness* that comes with the frustration of the extinction burst right before you quit—right before the "extinction" of the pen-shaking behavior. Trainers have found that sometimes—if they withhold treats from an animal who had previously been rewarded for a behavior—the animal will get *extremely frustrated* and will engage in *higher, superior, or more novel or creative behavior* that can then be jackpotted and reinforced.

The classic example of this in Pryor's books is of a dolphin that doesn't get rewarded for a jump, and then jumps really high, or does a back flip, or something wild like that. Of course, the risk is that—if you frustrate the animal too much—it will simply quit on you. Working with an individual animal, you rapidly get a sense of how much creative energy you can get out of it and what its tolerance for frustration is. However, the extinction burst can be a really powerful training tool if properly employed. Most trainers apparently believe that an animal needs to get a little frustrated before it gets really creative, or before it tries something really novel or superior. Thus, you can actually train for higher and more creative performance by allowing the animal to become a bit frustrated, and then waiting it out while it thinks up something to try.

I had my own first and rather startling experience with an extinction burst teaching Willow to retrieve. I had just finished reading Pryor's *Don't Shoot the Dog*, which explained how to teach dogs to retrieve Frisbees—not so different from teaching a dog to retrieve a tennis ball—or so one would think. I had wanted for some time to teach Willow to retrieve because each morning there was a local black Lab who followed us home after our walks. This dog, whose name was Jake, belonged to a neighbor and was getting on in years. He had rum hips, and a dull black coat, and matter in the corners of his rheumy brown eyes—but he still carried a tennis ball proudly everywhere he went, and his nose was still keen. (No doubt the reason he followed us home was that he could smell the dog treats in my pocket.) In any event, we had fallen into a routine where Jake would follow us home from our morning walks, and when we reached home, I'd throw the tennis ball for him a few times in our yard—a game Willow just watched—and then I'd give Jake a cookie and tell him to go on home. Jake seemed satisfied with this, and would trot home, usually after a dip in our kiddie pool.

For a long time, I had wanted to get Willow to join in our ball chasing game. It seemed like good fun, and Willow and Jake liked each other quite a lot and would snoozle each other affectionately each morning. The trouble was that Willow hated holding the ball in his mouth. Whenever I tried to give it to him, he'd just drop it, his mouth puckering slightly, spitting it out like a dead piece of gum—*Ptu*. And so, during my games with Jake, he would just stand there and bark at us, and refuse to participate—though often he would run back and forth with Jake (and try and steal the dog treats I gave Jake for bringing the ball back). Karen Pryor's books, though, gave me fresh hope that Willow could be trained to retrieve using a clicker.

And so, a couple of days after finishing my reading, I went to our living room on an afternoon when Willow was hanging out there, bringing with me a tennis ball, my clicker, and some jerky treats that Willow especially liked. Willow saw the clicker and leaped to his feet and started barking at me. He knew *this* game by now. Since we had already been working on heeling, I think he expected that's what we would do, but instead of heading for the backyard, I sat down in an armchair with the tennis ball in my lap. Now I had his attention. He came and stood in front of me, and nipped at the clicker. *Let's get to it*, he seemed to be saying. The trouble was, he didn't yet know what it was we were getting to.

My initial plan was to give Willow the tennis ball and then click him for holding it in his mouth, eventually stretching out the amount of time I required him to hold it. This didn't work at all, since he treated any attempt to place the ball in his mouth as forcing him to do something distasteful—no matter how gently I did it. I knew by now from working with him that he was sensitive to such things—to any force or punishment, and I knew that he would react negatively to anything he viewed as unpleasant. This needed somehow to stay a fun game. I couldn't apply any force or pressure at all. He would have to do it himself.

I tried another tactic. I threw the ball out several times from my chair, thinking he might run after it and pick it up. No dice. The best he would do was to nose it. He did this repeatedly. It felt as if we were at a stalemate. I would throw the ball, and it would roll and stop, and Willow would watch it, and then go and sniff at it. And that was it. This was quickly frustrating both of us. I wasn't getting anywhere, and Willow wasn't getting any jerky treats, and he was starting up his frustration barking at me, a shrilly pitched tone that was hard to listen to.

I decided at that point to reward him just for touching the ball. That wasn't picking it up, but it was the closest thing to it that I was getting. And both Cheryl Wells and Karen Pryor had said you couldn't expect perfection. You had to click and treat what you had, and then go from there. I sighed, and threw the ball again. Willow pounced after it, and then sort of bit at it, as he had done with the coffee cup lid in our targeting game. *Nipping the ball. Well, that was closer*, I thought. I clicked and treated Willow, and threw the ball again. We did this a few more times, but now Willow seemed only to be playing the target-touch game with the ball, occasionally taking a nip at it, but otherwise just touching it. *So now what?* I wondered. I could almost hear both Karen Pryor and Cheryl Wells lean over my shoulder and whisper, *Now you raise your criteria.* And so I stopped treating Willow just for touches or nips.

I threw the ball. He nipped it. No treat. His head flew up, and he leveled his gaze at me. *Now what's she doing?* He nudged the ball with his teeth. Still no click. He started barking at me again with that frustration pitch. Suddenly he turned and bit the ball hard, lifting it into the air. Closer! I clicked and treated this. Soon I had him picking up the ball in the air—real progress, I thought. Still, each time he would spit it right back out again, and he still seemed to have no idea of moving it anywhere. In fact, I couldn't get him to hold it long enough even to bring it an inch or two toward me. He would lift the ball a foot, and then spit it out again like that piece of gum. *Ptu. Get this thing out of my mouth.* Still, just getting him to pick up the ball seemed like progress, and so we quit there for the day. Sue Reed had drilled into me to *train in short sessions* and *know when to quit.* So I rewarded the pick up a few more times, and then told Willow what a good doggie he was, and we stopped. He seemed satisfied. So was I.

What I didn't realize was that we would stay stuck at this stage for days. I still couldn't get Willow to move the ball anywhere. During our games with Jake, he would now chase the ball alongside the old Lab, but if he beat him to the ball—which he often did, being much younger—he would just bite it, lift it, and then drop it right away. At which point Jake would calmly pick up the ball, bring it back to me, and get the cookie. This was terribly frustrating for Willow. He could see that Jake was getting a treat and he wasn't. To this day I still don't know if during this period he was putting 2+ 2 together and deducing, *The dog who brings the ball gets the cookie*, and he was just resisting doing it because he didn't like holding the ball in his mouth, or if he genuinely wasn't sure what I wanted.

And so we found ourselves on yet another afternoon in the living room, Willow and me, with clicker, treats, and ball. I rewarded him twice for biting and lifting the tennis ball, and then stopped rewarding him. I decided that I was not going to reward him any more that day until he moved the ball. He bit and lifted the ball repeatedly, each time spitting it out. He looked at me, barked with frustration, clearly was about to quit. Then suddenly I got that extinction burst out of him. He lifted the tennis ball with his front teeth, shook it hard like a sock, and then let it go. With the force of the shake, the ball made a high arc in the air and—probably by accident—came flying toward me. I reached out and caught it, and jackpotted Willow, praising him like crazy. "Good boy, you got me the ball!" I threw it again. Willow went to the ball, lifted it again, and spat it out. Again frustration, no treats. Then, in an odd little moment, he picked the ball up, shook it a little again, but this time kept the ball in his mouth, trotted a pace or two toward me, and dropped it near my feet. Lots more treats for that. We quit there, and I wasn't quite sure what we'd accomplished. But the next morning when I threw the tennis ball for Jake, Willow seemed suddenly to know exactly what to do. He chased down poor old Jake, beat him to the tennis ball, grabbed it in his mouth, and raced back to me, and spat it out at my feet—*Ptu*. It was exactly as if he were saying, *I still hate the taste of this darn ball, phooey, but I'll take that handful of nice cinnamon dog treats, thank you. We both know they're mine!* After that, ball chasing became a great game for us in the morning, with the two dogs racing each other for the ball, each trying to beat the other for the cookies. Since Willow was younger and faster, I'd sometimes reward Jake just for running to the ball, even if he didn't get there first.

Then, one morning a third dog followed us home from our walk, a big pretty golden retriever with a head like a lion's, named Gromit. I had occasionally seen this dog walked in our neighborhood, and his owners apparently lived a couple blocks away, near Jake's family. Gromit wasn't usually out in the mornings, though, because his owners were a childless couple who both worked all day. Also, I'd heard that they had an electric fence. When he and Jake both followed us home, I figured that Gromit had broken out of his e-fence, as dogs sometimes will do, deciding to take the shock for their freedom. I intended to take him home after our morning retrieve game. (I would later learn that Gromit's owners were actually out of town on vacation, and that he was staying with Jake's family.) At any rate, I threw the ball for Willow and the two retrievers in our yard for a while, all three dogs having a grand time. With three dogs bent on cookies, though, there was more scrambling than usual, and soon Jake's tennis ball had skittered off into the bushes, and I couldn't find it. So there I was, standing in the yard, with three big happy panting dogs gazing attentively at me and waiting for me to throw something.

"I'm sorry, boys," I said to them, holding out my arms in a shrug. "I can't find the ball."

At the word *ball* they became visibly more excited, jumping around with happy expressions, hot dog breath filling the air.

"No ball," I said, as if they could understand English. They wagged their tails furiously. "I guess we'll have to use a stick," I said.

At the word *"stick,"* both Willow and Jake dove for sticks on the lawn and came back tossing them in their jaws. Gromit just stood there waving his tail, a blank look on his face. At the time I remember thinking, *That's so funny. Willow and Jake really do know English, at least a little.* I also thought, *Boy, is Gromit dumb.* After reflecting on it, though, what I think really happened was this: Jake and Willow both lived in homes with kids and therefore had good play vocabularies. They'd both had sticks thrown for them a million times and knew the word "stick." Gromit, on the other hand, lived in a house with only adults who probably spent far less time playing with him, and so he didn't know what a stick was. The thing that was a bit jolting for me was that both Jake and Willow had learned very well an English word that nobody had consciously taught them.

I began to wonder how many other words they knew. It was interesting that they couldn't absorb "no ball," though they clearly knew the words "no" and "ball." I have since noticed that dogs seem to lack any notion of syntax. Words in combination mean little to them. However, they seem to be able to understand quite well single words with a specific physical context, such as "cookie," "dinner," or "stick." I'm sure most dog owners have observed this about their dogs—I'm not breaking any new ground here—I had just never especially noticed this fact until that day. Now that I'm aware of it, I try and use all sorts of physical context words with my dogs that I think they will be able to add to their doggie vocabularies. My dogs know to "wait" before crossing the street, that "walkies" means going outside for a walk, and "home" means we'll return home. And the word "cats" will send Willow charging around the yard looking for where the kitty went.

TEACHING THE DOG TO THINK

One of the things I started to see around this time—as Willow and I really began to use our clicker—was that Willow's own individual nature was very much affecting the progress of our training. As we employed the clicker more and more, I began to see that Willow was actually quite slow to try new things, at least as compared with some of other, more lively and experimental dogs in our class, like little Gizmo. I began to reach the conclusion after a time that this really was a function of his individual dog personality. Gizmo would charge ahead and try all sorts of new behaviors—yet he was almost uncontrollable, and it was hard to get him to do the same thing twice. Willow, on the other hand, was a follower, not a leader. He wanted to be lured, shown, led. It was hard to get him to try anything on his own. He wanted instructions. Yet once you had established a trained behavior with him, he was rock solid, and would repeat it for you over and over, spot on perfect. It was interesting for me to see such different personalities within dogdom. *How like people they are*, I remember thinking. *How utterly individual and themselves.*

In retrospect, I find all of this clicker training very interesting, especially my experience teaching Willow to retrieve—both in observing language skills in dogs, and also in seeing how much I had to frustrate both Willow and myself in order to get Willow to try something new—to do something novel and different with the tennis ball. It is fascinating to me that in order to get a creature to try something new and better, you often need to frustrate it. Nor does this seem limited to animals.

These days I teach creative writing to adults, and I have certainly seen the same phenomenon in my writing students.

The students who come to my workshops often have a very limited range of strategies and approaches that they use in their writing, and part of teaching them to be better writers lies in getting them to try new techniques and to expand their repertoires. I usually get them doing writing exercises to make them practice new skills that they tend otherwise not to use on their own. The exercises start them off on the right foot, getting them to "do things right"—performance that I can then reinforce through praise and positive discussion. The exercises also help my students break down many of the harder tasks involved in creative writing into smaller sets of learned skills that they can apply when they get back to their own writing. But my human students—as they begin absorbing these new skills—often seem to experience a great deal of frustration, or even depression, frequently right before their writing takes a big leap forward. Sometimes they even get mad at me, as if there's something wrong with the time-tested exercises I'm giving them, or as if it's my fault their manuscripts aren't improving quickly enough. It is interesting to me as a teacher to know that head banging, temper tantrums, and even outright anger may be part of what you must inevitably expect whenever creatures—human or animal—are learning, and especially when they are being asked to try something novel, creative, or new.

What I find so interesting about the work of Karen Pryor, and of the many talented agility trainers practicing today, is that they make it clear that you can actually *train for creativity*. You can teach an animal or a human being the habit of trying out new and different things, of experimenting with alternate approaches and solutions—whereas most of us tend to fall back on our same old habits and strategies most of the time. The way you teach an animal or a human to be more creative is that you frustrate it by refusing to reward the old ways that have worked before. You have to *stop rewarding* those same old approaches and solutions, and then get out of the way while the human or animal has a little tantrum or fit. Then he'll offer you something really novel or extraordinary. Or, alternately, he might quit on you.

That, I'm sorry to say, has also happened to me as a teacher. Students get frustrated, quit, drop out of class. They don't want to do the writing exercises; they don't want to practice the new skills. It's too hard, too different from what they are used to. The difficult part I find as a teacher is in balancing how much encouragement and praise the student needs, with how much frustration he or she can take.

VI. Teaching the Human to Think

Seventeen

As is probably clear from my discussion of frustration and creativity, at some point along the way I began applying all of this positive training I had learned to humans. However, I have to say it took a while for me to get there. Until I read Karen Pryor's books, it was all pretty much dog training to me. There was something about reading up on the theory, though, that broke the floodgates in my head, and made me see that a lot of what I had been doing was fully applicable to teaching humans—and particularly to improving my own rather dismal parenting skills. I don't know why I suddenly saw the light. Perhaps it was because Pryor made clear in her books that none of this was species-specific, and that her training methods could be used just as well on a human or a scallop. So it was that I found myself one evening standing over Daniel, trying to get him to do his homework, and I experienced one of those funny gestalt switches, where suddenly you see everything a little differently.

Daniel, at the time, was in second grade, and he was just beginning to get real homework for the first time. He was attending a Montessori school, and there wasn't even a *lot* of homework, but several subjects were assigned on a weekly basis, and somehow it would all pile up and have to be done the same night—generally a Thursday night, since everything was due on Friday. The way I had handled this previously was to inflict punishments. You don't get your homework done, no TV for the next two nights. If this isn't all done by tomorrow, no Gameboy for a week. My son is a sensitive, dreamy fellow for whom time has a way of drifting past after school, and all that this threat of punishment was doing was resulting in even more procrastination, and then in crying and tantrums when the horrible punishments were inflicted—no matter how mild they actually proved to be. I would find myself standing over my son like an ogre, saying hurtful and often untrue things, such as, *Your father and I always got our homework done*, and *You are going to ruin our good family name. We are a family that does our homework!* We would both end up crying, and the homework would not get done. This, then, was the habit we had gotten into.

It was on one such Thursday night that I was articulating for my son—tears in both our eyes—some such escalating scale of punishments: no TV, no Gameboy, no video games for a day, a week, a month. No dinner. (*No dinner? Was I really prepared to do that to my Daniel?*) Having just read Karen Pryor's books, though, I was suddenly struck by how similar all of this was to the escalating punishments I used to inflict on Willow. It was the same kind of coercion and rigidity. It all had to be done *right now* and *perfectly*. If not there would be stare downs, scruff shakes, choking with a chain collar. I knew now, though, much more about how to get Willow to work with and for me. *Good lord*, I thought suddenly, *I'd never do this to a dog*. I remember feeling rather shocked with myself. I looked down at my sniffling son and thought, *If this was Willow, what would I do?* The answer of course made me review all that I had learned.

First of all, break it down into small manageable steps, amply rewarded. And stop expecting perfection. He might not get *all* his homework done tonight. However, at the moment, *none* of it was getting done. What I needed to do was deal with the reality of what was happening. I needed to get Daniel moving in the right direction. I needed to ignore the bad behavior and reward anything that moved *toward* getting the homework done. And the rewards I gave him needed to be something that he really wanted. I needed to deal with him *on his own terms*.

My son that night was struggling with writing a two-page essay on a story he and his Montessori class had read in their *Great Books* readers. He had written only two or three essays before in his short life and was not an experienced essay writer. "Tell ya what," I said cagily to him—I was thinking of the bag of Reese's miniature peanut butter cups I had secretly stashed in the freezer earlier, for my own consumption, after grocery shopping. "You write the first paragraph of the essay," I said, "and I'll get out some mini peanut butter cups I happen to have." Now, saying this, I had to take a giant leap of faith. I had to ignore all of the well-meaning parental advice that you've heard from all the experts who say never, ever, bribe your kid with food. But, really. The situation was desperate. Even if we got through the essay, we still had two pages of math problems to do.

"You've got peanut butter cups?" my son said suspiciously, wiping his eyes with his sleeve, not believing me. I usually only bought bags of candy at Halloween. "When did you get them?"

Well, I explained a bit more boldly, I'd gotten them while grocery shopping, and I meant to keep them in the freezer for myself, but he could have three for every paragraph he finished.

"Five," he said.

"What?"

"Five peanut butter cups for each paragraph."

We agreed on four. "But I'll take away one," I told him, "if it's messy."

He wrote the first paragraph, three entire sentences, in remarkably good second grade printing and—I have to add—in about a minute and a half. Really. Maybe less. Half a minute. Apparently this mental block was about procrastination and motivation, not about ability or experience.

"Okay, where are my peanut butter cups?" he demanded. He chewed them still gazing at me rather suspiciously. Was I really going to give him even more candy if he did more homework?

Another paragraph, four more mini peanut butter cups.

The essay was soon done, and my son was no slow learner. "What do I get for the math?" he said coolly—as cool as only a seven-year-old can be.

He negotiated for an hour of TV, and then to stay up half an hour late to play Gameboy in bed—usually we never allowed video games at bedtime. Clearly I had created a monster. But the homework was entirely and painlessly done, and in lightning speed. I could now sit down with a glass of merlot and read the *New York Times*. And my son and I were on great terms. I got a big hug and a kiss from him on his way to the TV. "Thanks for the homework help, Mom," he said with disturbing blitheness.

Going for my glass of wine, I found my husband snickering in the kitchen, where he was doing our dinner dishes. "You'd better hope he doesn't start asking for money," Steve said. "You're a lousy negotiator."

"Don't worry," I told him. "Pretty soon we'll put him on a variable reinforcement schedule." My brain raced to try and figure out how that would work with a kid instead of a dog. Then I thought, *Dishes, now there's something that needs reinforcing.* I slid up to my husband where he was bent over the sink, up to his elbows in hot water and suds, and slipped my arm around his waist. "Thanks for doing the dishes," I said, in a low seductive tone, and gave him a long slow passionate kiss.

"Was that a reward?" he murmured, his eyes half closed.

"Mmmm. Hmmm."

"I think I like it." Suddenly he turned his head, his eyes snapping open. "What do you propose we do about him?" He was looking at the cat, who had hopped up on the counter and now had his face buried in a large pan that held the remains of our dinner—a spicy fish and rice dish.

Now I know a behavior I want to extinguish when I see one. *Any problem with switching a cat off getting up on the counter to eat your dinner? Nope.* "Time for a correction!" I cried, and reached with gusto for the squirt bottle we used to mist the plants, and let the cat have it.

Okay, I admit it. A little mild "aversive stimulus" can be sort of fun now and then.

I no longer have to bribe my son with candy. He is older now, and the rewards he wants as a teenager are bigger and fewer. Downloads on his iPod, cash to go out with his friends. The lure of a new laptop if he can bring up his spring term grades. On the other hand, he knows the routine and is more demanding. Faced with a big project for school, he will turn to me, slip his arm around my shoulders (he's taller than I am now), and say, "Mom, I think we need to reward me to get me through this." He will usually have something in mind that costs money. Still, he is a good student—not always an A student—but a good student. And he is extraordinarily creative. His teachers remark on it. And our own relationship is much better. I think positive reinforcement is helping us survive adolescence. I no longer need to badger, threaten, or yell. Daniel and I are on the same team now. We both want him to do well and to earn the goodies. And I can't help but think this is sending my son a good message: *Work hard and you win the rewards.* That seems to me a much better message than, *If you don't get your work done, the boss will punish you.*[6] The human will is a formidable thing. You don't want to work against it, and certainly not with a teenager.

I regret now the many punishments I doled out when Daniel was younger. I think that my punishing and threatening him for not doing what I wanted had an incredibly corrosive and negative effect on our relationship. It's very hard being a parent. It's damn hard to get anyone in this world to do what you want, let alone your own kids, who half the time are out to challenge you. But I now believe that it takes a huge amount of yelling and screaming to get the results that even a small reward will bring. But more than that, there's a price to

---

6. I should note here that a debate has been raging for years among educators and psychologists over whether rewards should be used to motivate human students. Relatively little attention appears to have been paid, however, to what actually stimulates excited learning in students of different ages, or how "operant" training theory might be employed to foster communication with students and involve them more in their own education. Also, there has been little discussion of how the withholding of rewards might be helpful at certain stages in keeping a student's attention and in fostering creativity. What is absolutely clear to me, though, being the mother of a high school student myself, is that the rigid grading policies in use at most schools today can stifle even the most capable student.

pay for the threats, the yelling, the punishments. If I yell at my son for not doing his homework, if I threaten to take away his Gameboy, there's a real cost to our relationship. If I snipe at my husband for failing to help with the dishes or take out the garbage, something corrosive happens between us.

I wish I had learned all of this before Daniel was seven years old. I think that when he was younger I threatened too much and handed out too many time outs. I never spanked him, thank goodness, but I was far too rigid. I expected adherence to fixed rules, and right now—this minute. I think I was, again, falling back on old habits and styles that I was used to.

Unfortunately, before becoming a mother, I had practiced law for several years, work experience that had taught me very punitive and coercive styles for making people do what I wanted. I had learned to manipulate and push people around. And not just opposing counsel, either, but also the support staff. I would browbeat secretaries and paralegals to get work typed or out the door to be filed. And I think that I had brought some of these poor interpersonal habits home with me, to motherhood, so that my first reaction when Daniel didn't do his homework was to threaten him with retribution, or to say nasty things—rather than to try and understand what was holding him back, or what would help him try harder. There was no room for lower expectations, or for *just get started*. With these nasty, coercive tactics, I was probably modeling behavior that I had observed in older attorneys around me, but I think that I was also, in my work life, pretty inexperienced and naive about other people, and the range of my interpersonal skills was extremely limited. It was hard for me to learn more gentle and effective ways of getting people to do what I wanted—but that person was now my child—and on some level I think I knew that I was doing something bad, and was ripe for some rather painful insight into my own behavior.

Today I understand the value of *approximation*, of *shaping*, of just getting started with small successes and then building on them. Of working with what you have, and then going from there. I am also a kinder, better parent. My son has told me as much. He came home one day from having been over at a friend's house, and this friend had been chewed out by his mother for something routine, homework not getting done, a dirty room, something like that. When he got home, my son told me about this, and gave me a big hug. "I'm glad we work on rewards in this house," he said. "I'm glad you did dog training, Mom."

Eighteen

I should say here that one of the most powerful tools I have found for gently improving the behavior of human children is something I first heard Sue Reed talking about in agility class, and that Karen Pryor discusses at length in *Don't Shoot the Dog*—Namely the concept of "training an incompatible behavior." The idea here is that, if a person or animal is doing something bad or negative, you instead get him to do something positive that is inconsistent or incompatible with the bad behavior. For example, to control the din of screaming kids in the car, you can get everyone singing the same song. Similarly, bedtime rituals like reading stories are used by wise parents to thwart other unwanted behaviors, such as refusals to go to bed, fears of the dark, or endless requests for water or snacks. The best teachers and parents seem to know this almost instinctively. My son's fourth grade teacher used to regain control of her class after recess by training her students to fall silent and put their hands on their heads at the tone of a bell. Kids who weren't paying close attention to this game would be the last ones talking and laughing, and they would look foolish to the other children who were by then standing silently with their hands on their heads watching them. The kids who were still making noise would become the objects of ridicule, making compliance that much more likely.

With people or with dogs, there are as many positive behaviors to encourage as there are bad ones to get rid of. At the office, team-building exercises such as constructing Lego structures together can help undo corrosive office politics by forcing employees to work together cooperatively. And gum chewing can help you quit smoking. That is why you always hear the best motivational trainers like Sue Reed and Karen Pryor saying that you must "train the good behaviors and ignore the bad." Focusing on the bad conduct that you want to eliminate just tends to get you into a cycle of punishments and shouting, "*No!*" On the other hand, a little creativity in dreaming up positive incompatible behaviors to train can save you a lot of yelling and screaming. And it can be great fun. It's so much better to sing "Ninety-nine Bottles of Beer" in the car than it is to yell "shut up" a hundred times.

In the end, training an alternate behavior has proved the solution to nearly all of Willow's most difficult behavior problems, such a barking in class and chasing joggers and bicycles. With Willow's barking in class, for instance, the attention games I was doing were working well in getting him not to bark while Sue was providing instruction. The trouble was that I was so busy distracting Willow that I was missing nearly everything she was saying. Eventually I brought this trouble up with Sue, and she said, offhandedly, "Oh, just put him in a down-stay. Dogs don't like to bark while lying down." This turned out, actually, to be perfectly true. It's hard for a collie to get up a head of steam barking when he's lying down. So once I put Willow in a down-stay position, he would usually bark once or twice and then lose interest in making noise. So thereafter, I simply trained him to hold a long down-stay in class through periods of instruction. We started with short stays and gradually rewarded longer and longer stays, until eventually he would hold extended down-stays through all the dull parts of class in order to earn his reward. It all seemed so simple and obvious in retrospect that afterward I was a little angry with myself for not thinking of it.

We did a similar thing with joggers and bikes, both of which Willow loves to this day to chase. I trained him to hold an attentive sit with his eyes on my face while the jogger or bike went past. At first, I had to hold the dog treat right up under my chin to keep his attention on me, but the beauty of training him to look *at me* while holding a sit was that it placed the bikes and joggers out of his line of vision. When he wasn't looking at these exciting distractions, they were a whole lot easier to resist. Instead, he was looking at me and the cookie. Gradually I was able to fade the treat and put it on a variable reinforcement schedule. These days, even with our vigorous training long past, I can still go to the park with a dog treat in my pocket, and if we see a jogger or a bike, I can throw Willow into a sit-stay and tap my chin, and he will hold his focus on my face while the chasable thing—whatever it is—goes by. The only things we have run into for which this won't work are motorcycles and llamas. Fortunately, motorcycles are banned in most of the conservation areas and parks we frequent. However, there is a brace of llamas from the local Wildlife Rehab Center who do occasionally go for a stroll at one of the parks where we walk. If I see them coming, I put Willow on a leash. As with the horses at Sue Reed's equestrian arena, hoofed animals still set Willow off, and there is very little I can do about it. I have since learned that the big Scottish collies were bred as drovers, which means that they were supposed to bark loudly behind stock all day long, driving them to market. It is simply in his nature to bark at cows, horses, sheep, and—apparently—llamas. That's what he was bred for. Any training I do to try and get him to stop is working against everything in him. But that's okay— I no longer expect perfection of my dog. We have solved the big problems—joggers and bikes—and most days we do pretty well. People have often remarked to me, watching Willow holding one of his perfectly attentive sits while a jogger trots past, what an exquisitely trained dog he is. If only they knew, I always think, that such excellent control only comes through giving up the very idea of perfect control. It is a contradiction, a conundrum. And on the days when Willow breaks that perfect sit-stay to howl like a banshee at the llama clomping down the path, I shrug and laugh and snap on the leash. Willow isn't perfect. Who is?

Train an alternate behavior—it seems like such a simple thing: You don't want the kids yelling, get them to sing. You don't want the dog to bark, get him to lie down. So why couldn't I think of those things on my own? The same thing with our experience training leash walking: I didn't have to choke Willow to get him to walk on a leash without pulling. I could just refuse to move until he stopped pulling. Most of the training methods I had learned seemed, after the fact, like such simple, logical, and elegant solutions. Yet looking back and reviewing my training history, I can see that time after time I was unable to come up with any of them on my own, not without the advice of an experienced coach, and I began to wonder why that was. Why was it so hard for me to come up with answers to these problems that substituted a little finesse for force?

I have thought about this for a long time, and I think that there are probably many reasons, but for me the main ones are these: First, as I have noted, yelling or applying force can feel good, at least in the short term. You get to express your anger and frustration and reassert your position in the world. It isn't pretty, but I do think that's a lot of it, at least for me. And, second, even if you want to change, it can be very difficult to develop new habits of mind, new ways of thinking and being— so that you don't keep falling back on the same old things you've always done. It requires an extra effort of the brain to dispassionately screen out the noise of your own emotions, and ask, in a cool, rational way, *What's really going on here?* And, *What else could I do to change the dynamic?*

Finally, I think some people—and I put myself in this category—simply have trouble giving up the sense of control that comes with forcing and dominating in order to take advantage of these kinder and more effective methods. Perhaps others have had experienced this too—I can speak only for myself. I now think that I'm a bit of a control freak. Controlling and dominating a dog or a small child does seem to make me feel as if I were more in charge of my world, and I think this gives me the illusion that I can prevent bad things from happening.[7]

7. I think this sense of control issue is why a lot of adults, even when they begin to appreciate the benefits of positive training theory, have a lot of trouble really giving up using punishments or "corrections." There is a feeling that you aren't going to be effective, or perhaps that you're being overly "permissive." Most parents and teachers end up trying to use some hybrid of the carrot and the stick. They use *both* corrections *and* rewards. However, science is beginning to reveal to us that these two modalities— punishment and learning—activate two very different and incompatible neural pathways. The "corrections" end up "shutting down" the student from performing the very kinds of experimentation and excited learning that make positive teaching so powerful. Karen Pryor has an extended

Why am I like this? I suspect that some of it is innate, part of my personality. And some of it may be attributable to losing my father at a young age. I haven't talked about this yet, but a couple of years after we lost my poor Tippy, we lost my father, too. When I was thirteen, he was killed in a car wreck coming home late one evening from a business trip in New York. I'm sure some psychologist could probably link up my need for a sense of control with the loss of control I felt in my young life as a result of that event. Or perhaps it was coming of age without the security of having a father figure in the house. Whatever the case, I'm glad today that I know this about myself so that I can try and do something about it, and not inflict this part of myself on everyone around me, especially those I love.

I must, however, also confess my dirty little secret: these urges for control have not gone away with my new understanding. I still yell. Not all the time. Not as much as I used to. But I still do. Sometimes it still feels good to express my anger and frustration. I still need control. I have not fundamentally changed as a human being. If my son and his pals are shouting too loudly in the backseat, I still yell, "*Qui-et!*" With me the change is not in the yelling, but in what happens next. When the kids yell right back at me, "*Wha-at?*"—in exactly the same tone and volume that I have roared at them—I can see how foolish I have been, and that I have only added to the din. The mood stays lighter. We all have a good laugh and try to think what else we could do.

discussion of this, by the way, in her latest book, *Reaching the Animal Mind* (Scribner 2009).

VII. Sympathy

Ninteen

Willow and I completed Cheryl Wells' class with flying colors. We had utterly mastered the beginners' class, both the skills and the theory, and had been promoted to advanced beginners. We got a paper certificate as the proof of our accomplishment—as if we had graduated from kindergarten or something—which felt a bit silly, but also rather good. We had *earned* that little piece of paper. We wanted, of course, to continue with our training. The trouble was that it was now late fall and I had to sign up for my next semester of graduate school. I was reaching the end of my degree program and was having to complete some core requirements that I had avoided until that time in order to finish my master's. There was one literature class in particular that I could no longer dodge, and it was held only on Tuesday night, which was also the only night of the week that Sue Reed and Cheryl Wells offered their advanced beginners class. Since I would no longer have my Tuesday nights free for dog training, I now found myself having to seek out new agility trainers.

Someone in Cheryl's class recommended a well-respected agility judge who held weekend classes up in the Andover area. Andover was a long trip north of Boston for us, but this agility judge, Mark Phillips, and his wife, Annie Phillips, were offering an advanced beginners class on Saturday night when the traffic would be less of an issue than it would have been during the week. I was already going to be out two nights a week that winter for grad school classes, and I liked the idea of training Willow on Saturday nights when Steve would be around so that I didn't have to leave Daniel with a sitter for a third night of the week. Also, I was determined to stick with positive training methods, and the Phillipses were listed on the clicker training websites as well as the agility sites. And so I emailed them, and signed up, and Willow and I began trekking up to Andover Saturday nights for agility training.

My memory of that winter, driving up to Andover with Willow for dog training, is tinged with a sort of sad rosy glow. These were our last euphoric moments of training together before everything went wrong. It was a particularly cold and snowy winter that year, and I recall long drives up the expressway through ice and snow in a warm car that was humid with dog breath, the windshield fogging inside. North of the city we'd pull off an exit, slush kicking the undercarriage of the Outback, and do a drive-through at McDonalds to stock up on cooked hamburger for class. Willow became a real fan of McDonalds cheeseburgers that winter, and he'd start barking like crazy as soon as he spied the golden arches and smelled the hot grease. Then we'd drive out through the rolling snow-covered fields east of Andover, where Holsteins had once grazed but McMansions now sprouted.

The snow on the North Shore was several feet deep that winter—It is colder up there, not being sheltered by Cape Cod like the South Shore. And the snow seemed to cushion everything. The ponies and horses we saw along the back roads on our way to class were as shaggy as Andes llamas. Though the new training center was also referred to as an "equestrian arena," it could not have been more different from the place where Sue Reed held her classes. The new arena was a long low-ceilinged building with high cement sides and a row of tiny square windows along the top of one wall—and it appeared to be a converted cow barn. The shavings on the floor were damp and full of road apples on which the dogs always tried to gorge. And the equipment was nearly all homemade, hammered to-gether from plywood and PVC piping. Except for a small warming room at the front, the place was unheated, and we could see our breath as we trained. Fingerless gloves were very popular that training session, so you could handle your treats while still keeping your hands warm. The students were also a more democratic lot. The Phillipses had an affiliation with a local kennel, which directed ordinary dog owners to them for obedience and agility classes, and so this was no longer the "dog fancy" set we'd encountered at Sue Reed's place.

Willow loved training in the cold. He was now in his second winter, and he was really coating-up for the first time, getting that huge lion's mane and deep multilayered fur of the adult male collie. He was in his prime and fully plumed out, and he looked just gorgeous as he whisked around, running his drills with his golden feathers flying. If I'd been paying closer attention, I might also have noticed a slight stiffening of the joints of his newly matured frame, or a modest slowing of his body movements, but these things were still below my radar at that point. I do remember noticing that he seemed to get a little spacey toward the end of our hour-long classes—he'd lose focus and start exploring the sawdust for horse droppings. But we were working together very intensely, both in and out of class, and a lot of the dogs looked pretty burned out before class ended, and so I really thought nothing of it.

Our new instructor, Mark Phillips, was a robust, barrel-chested man with a thick red beard, a hearty laugh, and that wonderful calm animal trainer acuteness about him. He and his wife Annie were kindhearted people, apparently somewhat famous in dog training circles for dusting off jumpy little mutts from the pound and turning them into agility dogs. Mark's own dog was a homely brindled mongrel that had been badly scarred in some mysterious pre-rescue past. The mere fact that Mark had resuscitated this unfortunate stray made us all love him. We would have loved him anyway, because his class was so much fun.

The great thing about Mark was that, being an agility judge, he spent a lot of time creating agility courses for us. At a real agility trial, it is the trial judge who designs a new course for each new trial, and at nearly every class, Mark would have cooked up some short athletic run for us to try—probably to assist him in working out his own new course designs. We would run a few obligatory drills at the beginning of class, but soon we'd be zipping around the obstacles, zooming over planks, and whooshing through tunnels. For the first time, Willow and I discovered the thrill of speed. When you are running an agility course full tilt with your dog, things happen fast. There's no more time for treats. The commands you had been shouting fall away. You and your dog are reduced to that same minimal shorthand communication that Willow and I had first experienced in the woods—but now our maneuvers were more complex, and our communication had to be even more fast and sure. Willow would watch me with that laserlike focus of his, looking for a tip of the head, a nudge of the arm, or a set of the shoulders, telling him where we were going. That was all it took to show him which obstacle was next. We were flush off our clicker training, and this new level of quick agility work seemed to flow naturally out of our new rapport. I'd once heard Sue Reed say that there was nothing like running an agility course with your dog, and now—for the first time—I really knew what she was talking about. This was the most fun that Willow and I would have in all of our training.

We did have one small problem that winter. Willow was suddenly working up so close to my left side that sometimes it was hard to get him to go far enough away from me to take his obstacles. Mark dubbed him "Velcro dog" and told me that this was a normal stage for an agility dog to go through—getting overly dependent on the handler. He spent time giving us exercises to get Willow working farther away from me. Looking back at it, I think that I had probably aggravated the situation by doing all that close-up clicker-heeling work with him right before we hit this stage. But in truth, I didn't mind Willow working close in. I was a feeling a little overly dependent on him, too, and I found myself remembering how my old BC Tippy and I used to lean against each other in obedience class when I was a kid.

In addition to trying to get us to work farther away from each other, Mark also had us working to master the more advanced obstacles—the teeter and the weave poles. He made it clear that both obstacles were difficult to train, and would be easier to master if we had equipment to practice on at home. It was hard to get a dog weaving really well if you were only doing it in class once a week. The same was true with getting truly comfortable with the tippy teeterboard. And so our wintry yard in Marshfield began to fill up with agility equipment.

We still had our old planks, and now they were joined by a set of weave poles and a low seesaw, all of which I have to say got far more use by Daniel and his friends than by Willow and me that cold January and February. My son and his pals would play "dogs," and would tip the teeter back and forth with their feet, walk the planks with their arms held out to their sides, and cavort through the poles, and then give each other "cookies"— real cookies in their case, or small snowballs.

Weaving turned out to be relatively easy for Willow to learn. He loved being lured and led, and all I had to do was hold out a chunk of meat in front of his nose, and he would happily follow it, snaking his long collie body through the poles after my hand. He quickly got the knack of bending his long spine this way and that as he went around each individual pole. He would never have the lightning speed of a border collie, I thought, but he was slow and steady and got the job done. We practiced two weeks at home, and then went to class and performed a couple of weave pole runs to show off our new skill. I remember one of our advanced beginner classmates asking, surprised, "When did Willow learn to weave?"

"Gosh, I don't know," I said. "He just sort of caught on." And he had.

The teeter was not such a snap. In class, we practiced on a very low seesaw with a six- or eight-inch fulcrum. But Willow, being a sensitive, careful dog, always seemed to think he was doing something wrong when the plank moved under his feet. He began avoiding the teeter, and was even starting to look askance at regular planks again—to my dismay. But then one day we were out trail hiking, and Willow walked across an iced-over puddle. The ice suddenly buckled under his front paws, and a sheet of ice flipped down, with the exact same motion as the teeter. I treated Willow and praised him for this, generally making a big fuss out of what a good dog he was. I was figuring, *reward him for anything that moves under his feet.* Soon we were onto a new game—dashing around the woods on our walks looking for ice skimmed puddles to break. Fortunately, the South Shore of Boston was as icy that winter as the North Shore was snowy. Actually, most of our usual hiking trails were impassable. But Norris Reservation in Norwell had a long muddy trail with lots of icy puddles, and so we went there and played our new training game.

I can still see Willow in my mind, his golden coat grayed by winter light, shimmering in the foggy air, his tail up and waving like a flag as he dashes along the trail, hunting puddles as if they were small animals. He checks over his shoulder to make sure that I am coming, an ear cocked and listening for my boots slipping along the trail and my voice saying, "Good boy! That's it!" when he cracks the ice, and a sheet of it flips down. I wish today that we could have stayed that way, frozen in time, working happily together—but it was not to be. The cracks were already appearing beneath us. In fact, something had already happened that should have set off all of my alarm bells, but that had gone by—while hardly unnoticed—still as if it were an isolated event of no significance.

Shortly before Christmas that year, our house had been a flurry of activity. We were doing our usual pre-holiday rituals, putting up the wreaths and the tree, and baking cookies. I was sitting on the floor one afternoon, surrounded by paper and ribbons and engulfed by baking smells—I was wrapping gifts between batches of Russian tea cakes—when suddenly the doorbell rang. I could see through the window that it was the UPS man, haloed by snow, and I started to get up, assuming it was one of my Christmas mail orders arriving, or an early gift. I had been sitting in one position for too long, though, and it took a moment for me to unkink my legs before I could get up. As I was stretching, still sitting on the floor, Willow, who was lying nearby and just behind me, jumped to his feet, as dogs will do, rushing to see who's at the door. As he brushed past me, stirring scraps of red and green ribbon with his feet, he suddenly staggered sideways against me. His back legs seemed to go both limp and stiff at the same time, which looked very odd, and his spine arched strangely. I didn't know what was happening, but he was clearly in distress and was starting to collapse, so I gathered him into my arms where I was sitting to steady him. He fell down sideways into my lap, his body twitching and writhing in a *grand mal* seizure.

It was an awful moment, but it was over almost as quickly as it had begun. Willow got up, shook himself, and looked around rather furtively, as if he were being punished for something. I told him he was a good dog and soothed him, and he wagged his tail and hung his head sheepishly. I was naturally very concerned, and as soon as we had taken our packages from the UPS man, I rushed my dog to the one big high-tech animal hospital on the South Shore to be thoroughly checked out. Nothing turned up, however; Willow's health checks seemed completely normal, and so I took him home with me that night. They wanted to hold him overnight at the hospital for observation, but I knew Willow would hate that. The vets told me collies sometimes had seizure disorders, but that especially in the winter a seizure might be an isolated event brought on by a virus. I was told to watch Willow for any more signs of seizures, and that if he did turn out to have epilepsy, there were drugs that he could be put on to combat the symptoms. Of course, if he had epilepsy, it would be too dangerous for him to do agility, climbing high equipment and so forth.

Over the next few weeks, I watched Willow closely, but there were no more seizures that I could see. He still seemed to me active and healthy, and I never really thought about giving up our agility training. At the time, I did not connect the seizure he'd had with the spaciness and fatigue he seemed to be exhibiting at the end of dog training class. And so we went happily along, continuing to train with Mark Phillips, and having a ball both in and out of class. Our teamwork continued to grow smoother and more effortless, and Willow seemed, right up through the end of Mark's class, to be as avid for the sport as ever. What finally happened to change things was that we were doing so well we got kicked upstairs, into the intermediate class. Then everything went to hell.

Twenty

Along around late February, when Mark Phillips' class ended, Willow and I were promoted to a brief late-winter intermediate level class with Annie Phillips, still in the cow barn. This short four- or five-week session was to be followed by a longer intermediate level spring class outdoors, beginning in April, at the kennel the Phillipses were affiliated with. There would be more equipment once we were outside, we were told, and—for the dogs who were up to it—an effort would be made to start getting them ready for some trialing in the fall. I felt a little thrill go through my stomach when I heard this. I also felt a bit sick. I think on some level I already knew it wasn't going to happen for Willow and me.

We still had several more weeks in the cow barn, though, before going outdoors, and Annie told us she intended to use the time to teach us the ins and outs of intermediate level handling: We would be learning front and back crosses, which would allow us to switch which side of the dog we were running on; tight turns over jumps (or "wraps"); and fancy jumping formations, such as clover leafs and figure-8's—which the dogs would need to know in order to perform quickly and efficiently at a real agility trial. Both we and our dogs needed to learn to "read a course"—which is to say, recognize familiar course and jumping patterns that we were likely to encounter at an agility trial, where the handler would be allowed only a short course familiarization period, and the dog would not have seen the course beforehand at all.

Willow got into trouble almost from the moment we entered Annie's intermediate class. The jumps had now risen to 16–20", and Willow would take two or three of them, and then refuse to do any more jumping. He'd walk away, sniff at the cold, damp sawdust for horse manure, and refuse to look at me or come when called. I blamed Annie. Whereas Mark's class had been nothing but fun, Annie's class was the very opposite. With Annie's emphasis on handling, everything in this new class seemed to be done in slow motion, and most of the jumping was performed from a standing start. We would spend half an hour repeating the same jumping drill over and over. Jump, wrap, jump, wrap, jump, wrap. In my own mind, I was sure that Annie was setting Willow up for failure. It seemed unfair to me that she would ask a big dog like him to clear twenty inches repeatedly without any running start whatsoever. It didn't help that I also found her personally grating. Annie was a bossy, rosy-faced blonde—brisk and efficient—who always seemed to be in some indeterminate stage of pregnancy. I took an instant aversion to her, and, I suspect, she to me. By this time, I felt that I had developed a fairly sophisticated understanding of dog training, and of my own dog, and she seemed determined to contradict me at every turn. When I said, "You know, he's a big lug. I think he could use a head start," she would say, in a flat, confrontational tone, "No one else is having trouble."

This continued for a couple of weeks, and I was quite sure that the problem was with how Annie was running her class, and not with my dog. I cringe now when I look back at my training notes from this period. I was *sure* that all this handling stuff was no fun for Willow, and that it was affecting his attitude. I could fool myself for only so long. After the third class—a bitterly cold March night roofed by needles of stars—Willow looked rather flat-footed walking out to the parking lot, and then he refused to jump into the rear of the Outback. He just stood there looking into the open tailgate where he was supposed to go, and wagged his tail at me, but he wouldn't climb in. No amount of coaxing could get him to leap up into the car. I ended up having to lift my by then eighty-five pound collie into the back of the Subaru. It was something I would get used to doing over the next few years. So much for having an agile dog, I remember grumbling to myself, as I boosted Willow's big furry butt into the car.

At the next class, Willow continued to look stiff and flat-footed. He would jump, but only if we "got him jeeped up," as Annie put it, getting him excited and running around barking before asking him to perform. Annie, to her credit, took me aside after class—I'm sure this was hard for her to do given my own attitude toward her—and said, "Look, I think something's going on with Willow. You need to go and get him checked out."

"Yes," I nodded. By that point, I could hardly disagree.

We skipped the last class of the late winter session, and I made an appointment with a good local vet clinic, where there was a specialist in canine cardiology and internal medicine. Again, though, Willow's health checks all came back normal. He wasn't diabetic or hyperthyroid. He didn't have Lyme disease or any kind of systemic infection. His heart and lungs were clear, his liver and kidney function normal. I explained to the vet we saw, Dr. Luther, the trouble we were having trying to do agility, and he said, "Well, Willow seems healthy to me. Some dogs just don't like to do sports."

This statement seemed to me so off base that it made me mad. I'm afraid I gave Dr. Luther quite an earful. Willow *loved* agility. That wasn't the problem. At that point, I think I was pretty abrasive to everyone in my path. My dog was young and fit, and just a year and a half old. He loved working with me, and he loved agility. Why couldn't he do agility? Why wouldn't he jump into the car? I wanted answers, and not to hear that he didn't like the sport. He did. I was sure of it.

Dr. Luther suggested that we have one more health exam, this with another doctor at the clinic, Dr. Haywood, who had a specialty in orthopedics. He was booked up for several weeks, though, and we wouldn't be able to get in to see him until the end of April. The next intermediate agility session with Annie Phillips was beginning in mid-April, and at that point Willow had had about three weeks off, and he had seemed to benefit from the rest. Though he still wouldn't jump into the Outback by himself, his stiffness had seemed to recede, especially with the improving spring weather, and so I signed us up for the next agility class. I can't quite account today for why I did this. I think perhaps at that point I was still half out to prove Dr. Luther and Annie Phillips wrong—and half out just to stick with agility until someone told me we had to quit. We had come so far. It was hard to imagine giving up our training.

We actually had a couple more classes outside at the kennel with Annie where things seemed to go okay. Once we were outside on a green lawn, there was less emphasis on handling over jumps, and there were A-frames and planks for Willow to have fun on again. But then came an especially hot day, and Annie had set up a jumping combination. Willow, who had seemed to revive during the past two classes, ran the course Annie had laid out twice, then went into a tunnel in the shade, and wouldn't come out again. He just crawled into the dark tunnel where it was dim and cool, and when I called him, even rather sharply, he just gazed out at me as if to say, *You've got to be kidding. Jump a cloverleaf in this hot sun? No thanks.* I finally had to crawl into the tunnel after him and physically haul him out and take him home. After that, we didn't go back again. Annie was right. Something was going on with Willow, and now I was determined to figure out what it was.

Dr. Haywood was the kind of fellow my father used to call "a character." When he walked into the examining room at the veterinary clinic, I thought at first that he was an orderly. He was a thin balding man with wispy blond hair past his shoulders and a scruffy goatee. He wore the same flowered purple smock as the female vet techs, out of which poked wiry muscular arms, and he squinted at us through gold granny glasses, as if he didn't see very well. Most of the vets at this clinic came off as overly polished professional people, but this guy seemed like an aging hippie. He also didn't talk very much, and, when he did, spoke in extremely abbreviated sentences. Nor did he examine Willow in anything more than a cursory way, mostly just watching him as he moved about the examining room, greeting this new vet person, sniffing the corners of the exam table. What an odd guy, I thought, ready to discount whatever he said.

After he had watched Willow for a time, Dr. Haywood turned to me, and said, "Does he take a long time lying down?"

"What do you mean?" I asked.

"Does he go around in circles a lot? Before he lies down?"

"Well, yes," I said. Now that I thought of it, he did. I hadn't thought anything of that before.

"What about stairs," Dr. Haywood said. "Does he avoid the stairs?"

Again, I hadn't really noticed, but now that I thought about it, Willow *had* started sleeping downstairs in the past few months. I had just thought that he *liked* sleeping down by the front door, where it was cooler, with that hot coat of his. It hadn't occurred to me that he might not be coming up to our bedroom in order to avoid the stairs.

"What about slippery floors—doesn't like 'em, does he?"

I looked at this hippie vet, astonished. How did he know this about my dog? It was perfectly true that lately Willow had been having trouble with the slippery hardwoods in our house. He seemed to be making an effort to avoid them at all costs, walking on the oriental runners instead whenever possible.

"Er, yes," I said. "That's true."

"Bad knees," Dr. Haywood said.

"Huh?" I wasn't sure I'd heard him right.

"Bad knees," he repeated, with an air of finality. He handed me Willow's chart so that we could check out at the front desk.

"That's it?" Apparently it was. Dr. Haywood had already headed out the door to his next appointment.

The front desk told me that Dr. Haywood had written on Willow's chart the name of an orthopedic surgeon at the same veterinary hospital where I'd taken Willow after his seizure— in case we wanted to follow up on the diagnosis. Dr. Haywood had also ordered a series of X-rays, which we should take with us when we saw this new specialist, Dr. Bosworth.

We didn't actually get in to see Dr. Bosworth for a couple more weeks, and by the time we had our appointment, it was mid-June. The summer heat was already setting in, and Willow was again exhibiting signs of heat intolerance, panting hard and looking miserable on our morning walks, though I'd had his coat thinned to a light summer weight by the groomer. He also seemed to tire even more easily, a symptom I no longer dismissed. Dr. Haywood had recommended doing two or three short (fifteen to twenty minute) walks, rather than one long morning walk, since Willow appeared to be having some kind of joint problem, and so we did that, hiring a dog walker to come in midday to take him out for an extra walk. Mostly, though, he just seemed very low on energy. All of his youthful vitality seemed to be seeping out of him. By the time we got to Dr. Bosworth's office, Willow's inability to jump was beginning to seem like the least of his troubles.

When we arrived at the reception area for the big veterinary hospital, and said we had an appointment with Dr. Bosworth, there was a lot of giggling among the female receptionists and vet techs behind the counter. I didn't know why until we actually met this new vet. Dr. Bosworth looked like a movie star. He was tall and slim and athletic, with black hair and eyes, high sharp cheekbones, and a matinee idol's smile—truly the whitest teeth I have ever seen that didn't look fake. Someone joked that in a moment I'd be going in a room with him and turning out the lights, which turned out to be true, since we would have to look at Willow's X-rays.

Unlike Dr. Haywood, Dr. Bosworth did take a long time examining Willow, bending over him and moving each of his joints one by one through their full range of motion—which Willow tolerated with good grace, though I'm sure now that it must have hurt him. Shoulder, elbow, knee, foot. The doctor seemed to pay special attention to Willow's front legs and shoulders. "Willow's hips are okay," he told me at last, leaning back from my dog. "The trouble is in the front." He said that Willow's front knee and elbow joints were very loosely put together. That high-stepping show ring gait of his also meant that his joints had a greater range of motion or "flex" than was normal, which made them less stable and more prone to injury. "He certainly shouldn't be jumping." Willow also had a mildly dysplastic right elbow, though Dr. Bosworth said, "It's not that bad for a purebred dog. I've seen lots worse. You should see the Bernese mountain dogs I've seen." There was something in the way he said *purebred dog* that would later stick in my mind. "The real problem," he continued, switching out the lights and lighting up a series of X-ray screens on the wall, "is this." He slapped up Willow's X-rays on a screen and, with a fluorescent pointer, traced what looked like white yarn crocheted across the illuminated bones of my dog's front legs.

"What's that?" I asked.

"Willow has advanced arthritis," he said. "That's what this white stuff is, around the joints."

"Advanced arthritis?" I was stunned.

"How old did you say he is?"

"He'll be two in September."

"Yes, well…"

There wasn't much else to say. Dr. Bosworth showed me Willow's "crunchy" knee joints, and which one was the dysplastic elbow. We discussed pain relief and glucosamine tablets, which might potentially slow the course of the disease. Then I took my dog home.

Later that June afternoon I found Willow on his tie-out. Steve had put him out, and he had fallen asleep in his favorite spot in the yard, a cool station deep in the shade of a tall pine tree near the street where he could keep an eye on things and say hello to all the walkers and joggers who came along on their way to the river. Willow might be in pain, but he was still a sweet sociable fellow, and he had a lot of his own friends around the neighborhood—often people I didn't know but who knew Willow. He roused himself to greet me when I sat down beside him. He labored to his feet, nosed me, shook his golden coat, and then lay back down heavily next to me, emitting a groan.

I looked at his poor front knees, which must have been hurting him for months. The doctor had said the arthritis was *advanced*. How long had I been jumping this dog in pain? I felt a deep stab of remorse. I reached over, meaning to rub Willow's sore joints for him, now that I knew where the soreness was, but when I reached for his legs, he visibly recoiled, wincing away from my fingers. How insensitive I must have been to have missed this. I remembered back to Willow's very first difficulties with planks in Sue Reed's class—to the day he seemed to be limping. I wondered now how long his arthritis had been bothering him, and how much I had aggravated things by pushing him to do agility and to jump ever higher.

I think something happened to me that day, sitting there under the pine tree with Willow. I think I decided I wasn't cut out to be a dog trainer. Not really. I had done it again. I had failed in that most basic thing Sue Reed had taught me—to attend to my dog and really see what was going on. And I had failed not once, but for months.

I believe now that I was a bit hard on myself that day. I have since read that dogs, like wolves, disguise their pain so that they don't show their vulnerabilities to other pack members. Also, I had made what should have been a reasonable assumption: that a young purebred collie from a reputable breeder ought to be physically fit and in decent shape to play a sport. Still, I had utterly missed what was going on right in front of me, and this was a very painful moment for me, and one I perhaps needed to have in order to develop true sympathy for Willow. I had spent all those months priding myself on figuring out what was going on inside my dog's head, but the truth was, I hadn't done a very good job. I was still very much pursuing my own agenda, doing what I wanted to do, and not really caring to see what was happening right in front of my nose. I saw it all now, though, and I felt wretched. I would never again think of getting rid of Willow to pursue my ambitions. I have since come to appreciate that agility was the way I really got to know my dog and to communicate well with him. And in the end, I have come to see this as far more important than our degree of success.

With time and distance, I have found myself glad that Willow and I did have our fun times together, before his troubles set in. I didn't know it then, but the arthritis was only the beginning of Willow's health problems. He may have been in some pain when he did agility, but we truly did have grand times together, and I think that has made a great deal of difference with all that we've had to endure since then. There is a bond of trust and communication between us that we will never lose, and—when Willow has to go to yet another doctor visit—I can reward each prod and shot with a treat and a "good dog," and he knows that he's doing what I want of him, and that he isn't being punished. Despite numerous health problems, he's one of the few dogs I know who actually likes going to the vet, because—despite some discomfort—he knows that he will get to be a "good boy" and will see "Dr. Cookie."

Our agility career had its official end two months later, in August 2001, a month before the World Trade towers fell. I received a group e-mail from the Phillipses. They were enrolling a new intermediate level agility class for the fall, and I was still on their e-mail list. I sent Annie back an e-mail explaining about Willow's "bad knees," and told her we would not be continuing with our agility training. It was almost a year to the day from when I had first signed up for Sue Reed's beginner agility class. I got back a note of condolence from Annie. I still wanted to hate her just a little, but the note seemed genuine in its sentiments. She hadn't wished Willow's arthritis on him. She also hadn't wanted to train a dog that was clearly having trouble. After the fact, I could hardly blame her for anything she did or said. In the end, I came to feel grateful to her for stopping us. If her class had been more fun, if she'd given Willow the running starts I had wanted, it would only have prolonged the inevitable, and possibly could have caused further damage to Willow's joints.

Twenty-One

When did I begin to realize that Willow was badly overbred? Like my understanding that he was having trouble with his front knees, the picture emerged so slowly that at first I could hardly see it. There was the seizure. Then the arthritis. Then came the low energy and the sensitivity and fatigue. Soon there were food allergies and mucousy stools and diarrhea. More seizures. One day Willow was nibbling on his feet, and it turned out to be an outbreak of mange mites. By age two, all of his youthful energy had leaked out of him; by age three, he was nearly hobbled by arthritis; and by four or five, when I'd take him walking in the park, people would say, "Aw, what a pretty collie. How old is he?"—thinking I'd answer ten or twelve. When I told them how old he really was, they'd look shocked. "Wow, really?" Then I'd have to explain about the arthritis and so forth. Willow was, in effect, a very old dog at a very young age.

As his health troubles began to mount, I felt depressed and bewildered. It was bad enough washing out of agility, but I really hadn't counted on having a dog who was such a physical wreck at such a young age. I had another problem, too. This wasn't just any old purebred puppy that I could take back to the breeder and demand my money back. The trouble with doing agility and clicker training with a dog is that you really do get to know him, and you bond with him on a new level—you learn all about his personality and his emotions, and become a new kind of friends and partners.

Think back: I had watched Willow get competitive with that Rottweiler. I had seen how crushed he was when he was failing in Sue Reed's class, and his joy at coming back to be a star in Cheryl Wells's class. I had found out that he preferred to follow and not to lead, and that he was not terribly creative, but that he had a tremendous work ethic, and loved doing his job precisely and well. He also had a great sense of personal dignity, and he let me know when he didn't like something, such as holding a tennis ball in his mouth, or, at the end, jumping in pain. He was loyal, but within reason, and he seemed to have come to expect a certain level of respect from me, something that I had perhaps not anticipated would result from our training. Willow and I had, in short, become intimate companions and rather equal friends through our training—and it was now heartbreaking to watch him fall apart this way.

I did what I could. Took him to all the specialists. Researched every symptom. Nothing he had was fatal, but nothing was really treatable either. The things he was diagnosed with were, for the most part, these chronic, low-grade conditions for which there was only constant and consistent management: arthritis, mild colitis, mild epilepsy, low-grade mange, low energy, fatigue, intolerance to heat and stress. Except perhaps for glucosamine for the arthritis, there was no pill you could take for this stuff, just feed him a good diet, control the pain, and keep him moving.

I resorted, as many people do in these situations, to the Internet, looking for a magic bullet that didn't exist. Instead what I found were a lot of other purebred dog owners complaining about the same things. Of course, I had heard of the problem of the overbreeding of purebred dogs—I hadn't lived on another planet. But I had never encountered this trouble myself, and when it happened to me and my dog, it took a while for me to understand what was going on. In truth, it wasn't something that I really thought could happen to us. When I'd gotten Willow, I had done my research. I had started with a woman who was a top AKC collie judge and the unofficial dean of the Collie Club of New England, and she had referred me to a group of respected breeders who were producing sweet, smart, show-stopping dogs.

The day I really began to catch on, I found, on the Web, a site on collie health issues, which included a health survey of four hundred purebred collies. Except for hip and eye problems, which Willow has—fortunately—escaped, at least as of this date, the list of reported problems read like an itemization of Willow's symptoms: early onset arthritis, orthopedic disorders, mange, colitis, allergies, seizures. Shortly after that, I was reading forum posts, and saw another purebred dog owner complaining about similar conditions in a different breed of dog. There was a breeder on the thread answering back: She recommended glucosamine and avoiding grains. "Oh, and by the way, check your pedigree. It sounds like you have a dog that's too closely bred. Is he a line-bred dog?"

It took me all morning to find Willow's pedigree. When his registration papers had come from the AKC, they had seemed pretty irrelevant to our agility training, and so I had just tossed them in a shoebox somewhere meaning to retrieve them only if we needed them to register for an AKC trial someday. Suddenly I needed to locate them. When I did, what I saw made me sit down hard on the couch clutching Willow's "Certified Pedigree." The pedigree went back only three generations, but that was plenty.

Willow's father had been named—well, I'm not going to use the real names here—I don't want to get anyone in trouble. So we'll call Willow's father Ch. Green Acres' Copper Relic, or "Copper" for short, a champion sable merle collie. I had a picture of him—he was a gorgeous stunner of a dog, and Willow looked just like him. Copper had been bred to Willow's mother, who we will call Hill and Dale's Misty Morning, or "Misty," a small walnut colored female whom I had met the day we got Willow as a puppy. So that generation seemed okay on the pedigree. They hadn't bred a merle to a merle or anything obviously stupid like that—(breeding merle to merle can produce an albino pup with no eyes.) The trouble came with the next generation back: Copper and Misty both had the same father. I saw him in an instant—the troublemaker— we'll call him Ch. Scotch Legend's Copper Icon. Same registration number on both sides of Willow's pedigree. No doubt he was a winning champion stud dog to whom everyone wanted to breed. Willow was the victim of what these days is known as "Popular Sire Syndrome." Willow's dad, Copper, had—in short—married his half sister. The third generation back had all the duplications you'd expect from such a close breeding, many of the same dogs on both sides.

There was a name for this, I thought. It was called incest. No wonder Willow was such a wreck. He was a genetic wreck. I was furious. It was hard for me to believe that in this day and age someone would breed dogs this closely. Who were these people? Hadn't they heard of modern genetics? Until now, I had been assuming that Willow had just had bad luck, having all these low-grade health problems—that he was just a dog with randomly poor health. That happens sometimes. But it happens a whole lot more in families where inbreeding runs rampant.

The overbreeding of purebred dogs has become something of a public scandal in this country over the past ten to fifteen years. *Time Magazine* is credited with breaking the story in 1994 with its article, "A Terrible Beauty,"[8] which caused much discussion and controversy at the time. The article alleged that "as many as 25% of the 20 million purebred dogs in America—1 in 4 animals—are afflicted with serious genetic problems." The article laid the blame squarely at the feet of the breeding practices followed by AKC breeders and their breed clubs. Specific practices were singled out as vastly increasing the amount of inbreeding in particular breeds of dog, such as linebreeding, the practice of breeding close family members together in order to preserve certain desired traits—often some trendy or fashionable look, and "Popular Sire Syndrome," where a single champion male is used to sire a large numbers of litters, and whose genes thereby quickly come to dominate in a breed, resulting in many members of the breeding stock being closely related.

After the *Time* article came out, the AKC and its breeders fought back with their own propaganda campaign. They argued that they were being unfairly tarnished by association with puppy mills and other disreputable breeders—a few bad eggs who didn't care about the genetic quality of their dogs.

8. "A Terrible Beauty," *Time*, December 12, 1994, v. 144, n. 24:64(7).

A "reputable breeder," they said, would never knowingly re-produce a dog with genetic defects. In fact, they argued, the AKC and its breed clubs had gone to great lengths to elimi-nate from their gene pools any number of hereditary defects, such as retinal disease and hip dysplasia, introducing routine health checks for puppies and so forth. As a result, they said, AKC purebreds had far fewer defects in their genes than did the mongrels and crossbreeds touted as healthier by the *Time* article. This certainly was the line I bought at the time I got Willow. I thought I needed only find a truly good and repu-table AKC breeder in order to avoid these kinds of problems. I was now learning the hard way a very bitter truth.

The trouble, as I now understand it, is this: Purebred dog breeding—under the AKC or any other purebred registry—generally proceeds under what is called a "closed studbook" system. A certain number of "founding" animals are registered at the beginning or founding of a breed, and this becomes the breeding stock. All registered animals must be descended only from this stock in order to earn the title of "purebred." This works fine—to preserve desired traits and characteristics, such as collie sweetness and herding ability—so long as the founding population is large and diverse enough for a healthy breeding population. However, if something happens to nar-row this pool of genes too far, you get what is called a "genetic bottleneck." Population biologists have long known about this phenomenon. Wildlife experts have often encountered it trying to revive near-extinct species. If a gene pool starts to get too small, or if there are too few members left to establish a healthy breeding population, the members quickly become too closely related, too inbred, and the population simply "collapses" for lack of sufficient genetic diversity.

The real problem with many of the AKC breeding practices cited by the *Time* article is not only that they result in ill-advised incest breedings, such as Willow's, but also that they have the effect of whittling down the diversity of the gene pool as a whole over time within a particular breed. So for example, the overuse of a particular stud dog can, in just a few generations, result in most of the breeding stock being closely related to a single champion sire, causing a bottleneck. The gene pool is further narrowed by selection for particular fashions in how a dog ought to look that are so prevalent at AKC shows, and even ironically by trying to breed away from such unwanted genetic defects as hip dysplasia and collie eye anomaly. All of these practices remove diversity from purebred gene pools. The so-called "reputable breeders" believe that they can banish serious genetic threats from their bloodlines through testing, and that if they just eliminate every last genetic fault they will be able to breed close family members together without consequence. That is what pedigrees like Willow's are saying to us. Population genetics, though, teaches that there is no such thing as truly pure blood, free of all genetic defects.

Over the past few years, as the extent of this problem has come to light, many dog owners have turned to purebred crosses to restore "hybrid vigor" to their favorite breeds. These days the newspapers are full of advertisements for so-called "designer mutts," the most popular crosses being to poodles, producing adorable, lively curly-coated dogs of every size and shape with cunning names like "Labradoodles" (Lab/poodle cross), "cockerpoos" (cocker spaniel/poodle cross), and "schnoodles" (schnauzer/poodle cross). These crosses of purebred lines seem from anecdotal evidence to be producing healthier and more vigorous dogs than the dissipated purebred lines from which they were bred, while still preserving many of the desired characteristics. I recently saw a "puggle" (a pug-beagle cross), and had to wonder if collie-poos could be far behind.

Once I understood that I had a badly overbred dog, I did a lot of soul searching. I went through periods where I was extremely angry with Willow's breeder and with the AKC's closed studbook breeding practices, with the fashion trends, and the rage to propagate winning stud dogs. I wrote angry letters and e-mails to Willow's breeder that I never sent. I couldn't understand why someone would do this to my friend, Willow.

It has taken years for me to come around to a more sanguine view, and long discussions with my friend Debbie, another dog fancier, who previously owned a Portuguese water dog with Addison's disease, and who now has an apparently healthy standard schnauzer—though Deb does hold her breath a bit. We have for some time had a conversation going about why AKC breeders often breed their own stock too closely, because it's really the *breeders* we are talking about here—the AKC itself is just a *breed registry*. Some of it, Deb thinks, is that these breeders know their dogs and love them. "If you have two great dogs," she says, "you think, why not breed them?" I personally think perhaps it also has to do with access to the dogs. Purebred breeders often keep tight control of their breeding stock, and it isn't always so easy to get hold of a good bitch or dog to breed to, at least not one that isn't already closely related to your own. And I think it can sometimes seem better to breed to the dogs you know, rather than take a flyer on some unknown commodity from far off that might turn out to have all sorts of problems you don't even know about.

When I have complained loudly about "these AKC people," Debbie has turned to me several times and said, rather severely, "Look, you have to remember—*these people* you are talking about love their dogs as much as you do."

I am absolutely sure that is true. Perhaps it takes having your dear dog friend struck low by genetic disease to really get up in arms about closed studbooks and linebreeding. I have also, in the end, had to admit my own complicity—Like the AKC breeders I would criticize, I too wanted that same heart-stopping, lethal beauty when I got Willow. If I had looked more closely at him when I bought him as a puppy, I might have seen that he already looked a bit overbred, especially around the eyes. And wasn't I willing to overlook his troubles with planks, and with jumping, so that I could pursue my own plans and ambitions? Was I really so different from the breeders who bred Willow and who probably only wanted to produce pretty dogs that would win shows?

There is probably a lesson to be taken here, about the costs of trying to perfect nature. But perhaps the more important lesson has to do with how easily we humans overlook or dismiss the damage we are causing until it is too late. I worry, for instance, about the ever more sophisticated and powerful genetic techniques being used these days to alter food crops and livestock. If warning signs appear, will we simply ignore them because we are too full of our own ambitions and plans, some of them quite admirable? If my own experience is any teacher, the answer is probably yes.

Twenty-Two

This story has, I am glad to say, something of a happy ending. With a little experimentation, we have found a formulation of glucosamine and chondroitin made for humans that seems to have helped keep Willow's arthritis somewhat at bay. With this medication and a little chewable baby aspirin—which he seems to tolerate well—there are days when he still feels good enough to go on long jaunts. We try and get out in the woods at least a few times a week. Willow seems to do best out there, deep in the forest, where the footing is springy with moss and rotting leaves that cushion his sore joints. There he still bounds around like a puppy and is less hampered by his orthopedic troubles.

Once our training was over, we found that we had a lot more time to go walking together, and our trail hiking became as regular a part of our schedule as agility had once been. Out in the woods we discovered a funny thing. There were a lot of people out there with their dogs—men and women like me—people who saw their dogs as fully developed individual personalities who were worth spending time with. They were doing what the dogs really liked to do, go for long walks and smell things. It was good exercise for the humans, too. Willow and I discovered something else as well. That we each liked being out there in the woods with our own kind. It wasn't long before we were meeting up each morning with a revolving group of other dog owners and their dogs, and going for walks together. Willow had his dog pals, and I had my human pals. In the years since, these people and their dogs have become some of our dearest friends.

Willow seems happiest these days when he's out cavorting around the woods with his pals. He's always happy to see his friends, and, in fact, he tends to like the girl-dogs a bit too much, biting their fur, licking their faces, and prodding them inappropriately with his long collie nose. With his blond good looks and amorous ways, he has been dubbed "Fabio" by the dog-walking crowd. When we are all out walking together, several humans with our dogs, there is always a lot of merriment and high jinks. The dogs wrestle and play and chase each other, coming back periodically to frisk us for cookies. The people laugh and talk. "It's always like a big dog party, Mom," Daniel says, when he comes with us.

Sometimes it's a small scene or a minor event that shows you just how far you've come. For me that little drama happened a year or two ago, on a day in late winter. We were out with the dog-walking gang at the Widow's Walk Golf Course in Scituate, Massachusetts. Normally golf courses don't admit dogs, but Widow's Walk is owned by the town of Scituate, and when the golfers finish up for the season in November, the town lets the dogs in for the winter. It is a lovely golf course that takes advantage of its seaside location, and the course is built with a succession of holes set in native landscaping upon increasingly high dunes and ledges, until you come to the "Widow's Walk

Hole"—a rooftop green with a high line of sight past wind-stunted trees giving a panoramic view of the whole North River drainage basin, the river winding through the wheat colored marshes of Norwell and Marshfield, and out past the cliffs and beaches of Scituate to the blue Atlantic. Once the golf course closes for the season, this uphill hike is all ours for the coldest months of the year, and the dogs run riot across the fairways and frolic in the sand traps.

On this particular day, we had just returned from this heady walk, and were standing by our cars in the parking lot, our cheeks rosy with exertion, our eyes tearing from the cold, the dogs milling about us panting and tussling, when a pair of men arrived. Apparently they were just back from some winter golfing, and they were accompanied by two black Labs—one a grown dog and the other a scared little puppy with a curled spine and tail between the legs. Our dogs gave the two Labs their usual hearty greeting and all-over sniff—to the displeasure of one of the men, a large fellow who held the silver gleam of a putting iron in his hands as he called to his dogs from the edge of the grass. "Come," he shouted at the Labs. At the word *come*, the grown dog—who was standing a few feet away from me, socializing—shrank to the pavement of the parking lot, his chin extended and his head rolling sideways in a gesture of abject submission—but he moved no closer to his master, twenty feet away. In fact, this dog seemed almost immobilized by the man's voice. "Come!" the man roared again.

Until now my friends and I had more or less ignored all of this, and we were talking and laughing with each other, but the man's voice had now taken on a note of threat, and we began paying closer attention to what was happening. "Come!" the man shouted, ever louder, his face turning red. I remember looking first at the poor dog crawling on the pavement in front of me, and then at the man's angry face, and thinking, *Dear Lord, this used to be me.*

At this point, the man strode over toward our group, seized the adult Lab by the collar, dragged him a little way from us, and cuffed him hard between the shoulders. Our little group stood watching this, mouths open, mortified. "That's good," one of us said. "Hit him again and then he'll really want to come to you." I don't remember which of us said this. I'm guessing it was probably Catherine. At the time, she was the senior curator at an art museum, and she is used to being in charge. She is also the sort of person who does not lightly suffer bullies.

The man glared at her. He now had a leash on the adult Lab, and was turning his attention to the puppy, who was still skittering around the fringes of our group, being nosed by our dogs. As with the adult Lab, the man's shouting did nothing but make the puppy freeze and cringe even more. A little shudder ran through our group. We could all see where this was headed, and none of us wanted to see a puppy beaten.

All at once Susan, who is the most gentle and motherly of our group, began acting as if she had just spied the puppy for the first time. "Why, oh look!" she cried. "What a beautiful puppy!" She dashed forward and scooped the puppy upside-down in her arms like a baby, talking and cooing to it, and carried it back to the man. "You are so lucky," she effused, as she handed the puppy over to him, "to have such a lovely little puppy. Where did you get him? How old is he?"

The man looked a bit dumbfounded as he stood there with her, talking and admiring this little puppy of his. He could hardly hit the puppy now, since his arms were full of kicking, squirming, adorable Lab. The rest of us wanted to deck this fellow, but Susan had gently shown the man that he was behaving all wrong toward the puppy, that it was just a baby, and that he needed to treat it gently.

Standing there, watching Susan talking to this man, I probably felt more sympathy for this angry fellow than did my compatriots—for I gazed at him with great understanding and ambivalence. I had never struck my dogs, but not so long ago I had done just about everything else—scruff shakes, choking, stare downs, bullying. I knew that he felt his dogs were out of control, probably running toward the road where they might be killed, and that shouting at them and hitting them probably allowed him to express his own frustration, anger, and confusion. I also knew that his punishment of these dogs probably gave him a grim feeling of satisfaction, and of domination, and made him feel as if he was more in control of his life, and that he could prevent bad things from happening. I also knew, of course, that he was doing everything wrong. His threats of physical force toward his dogs, threatening and hitting them, had to be terrifying for the dogs, and a strong aversive stimulus. No wonder they weren't moving one inch toward him if they could possibly help it. How much better he would have done with a light happy, "Come!" and a handful of treats.

And then there was Susan, brilliant Susan, one of those people who know instinctively how to substitute finesse for force, smiling and praising what a nice puppy this man had, and turning the situation completely around, when the rest of us really wanted to hit the guy back. But of course, you couldn't do that. They were his dogs. And so Susan's way was better. The puppy wasn't being struck, the man was made to feel a bit ashamed and embarrassed, and who knows, maybe Susan would get around to mentioning that he might want to try taking the puppy to a good dog training class, where hopefully some gentler methods might take root.

In my next life, once I evolve a little more, I'm going to be more like Susan, and less like that guy with the Labs.

I once thought this story would end with me getting another border collie just like my old Tippy to compete with at agility, but somewhere along the line, I lost my ambition. In the end, I found that dog agility training had fundamentally changed my relationships with both my pets and my family, and that it had shown me a great deal about how to communicate with the very alien mind of a dog, if only I was willing to attend to him closely enough. I did eventually get another dog, but she was no BC. A neighbor died of cancer a year or two after our training ended, and I inherited a pathetic little pink worm of a Maltese, named Sadie. This tiny five-pound dog had been neglected after her owner's death, and had lost most of her hair from some combination of malnourishment and grief, and when we got her you could see right through her fur to her skin. She fell into my lap naked, emaciated, and riddled with worms, and harboring a raging urinary tract infection. My dog-walking friends couldn't believe I was carrying around this shivering, unpromising specimen at the Widow's Walk Golf Course and Norris Reservation our first winter together, zipped inside my down jacket. But as one of my dog-walking friends has remarked, "Sometimes dogs just happen."

We didn't know it then, but little Sadie would grow back a thick lush white coat, would gain weight and muscle, and eventually would prove not half bad at agility. No, I did not completely give up dog training, though I no longer have any desire to win ribbons. I have been training Sadie in order to develop the same kind of communicative and full relationship with her that I now have with Willow. It's probably good that I don't have any plans to compete with her. While scrappy and fit, Sadie has a bit of the terrier in her, and, like Gizmo from Cheryl Wells' class, is rather wild and hard to control. Fortunately, she has a real fondness for string cheese. That, though, is another story.

In the late winter of 2010, we had to say good-bye to Willow. He suffered a final massive seizure that left him almost completely paralyzed, and we had no choice but to put him down. He lives on, though, in the hearts of all who knew him.

About the Author

Kimberly Davis is an award-winning poet and the author of Kim's Craft Blog, http://kimscraftblog.blogspot.com/, a blog about creative writing craft and the writing life. Her work has appeared in many fine literary journals. Davis was the winner of the 2009-2010 James Wright Poetry Award. She lives in Hingham, Massachusetts, with her husband, Stephen Rider, and son Daniel. For more information about author Kimberly Davis, visit her website at http://kimberlysdavis.com/.

27155289R00141

Printed in Great Britain
by Amazon